The Great Fish Book

The Great Fish Book

A wonderful collection of fish recipes from the finest restaurants in Great Britain and Ireland

Absolute Press

Published by Absolute Press (Publishers)
14 Widcombe Crescent, Bath BA2 6AH.

First published November 1988
Reprinted December 1990

Editors **Nicki Morris**
Paula Borton

Cover printed by
Stopside Ltd., Windsor Bridge Road, Bath.

Phototypeset by
Sulis Typesetting, 4 Chapel Row, Bath.

Printed by
The Longdunn Press Ltd, Barton Manor, St Philips, Bristol.

Bound by
Hartnoll Bound, Bodmin, Cornwall.

Contents

Soups and Salads

Fish Soup Lynwood Style

Lynwood House, Barnstaple
Chef/proprietor Ruth Roberts

Serves 6

1 fillet whiting
similar weight cod, haddock, monkfish, lemon sole and cooked, shelled prawns
10 mussels (prepared as described on page 52)
4 fl. oz. (125ml.) white wine
1 pint (570ml.) water
knob of butter
1 medium onion, roughly chopped
4 mushrooms, sliced
¼ pint (150ml.) milk
3 medium sized potatoes, cooked
½ lemon, squeezed
1 dessertspoon chopped parsley
salt and black pepper
¼ pint (150ml.) whipping cream
croûtons

Place all the fish, except the prawns, in a pan with the white wine and water. Bring to the boil and then remove from the heat. Let it stand for 5 minutes before removing the fish and mussels. Reserve the stock. Melt the butter in a saucepan and, when sizzling, add the chopped onion and mushrooms. Gently cook for 5 minutes without letting them colour. Liquidise the fish stock, add the milk and the potatoes and then strain this sauce over the mushrooms and onions.

Remove any skin or bones from the fish and prise the mussels from the shells. Add the flaked fish and mussels with the lemon juice and parsley to the soup and season to taste. Add the prawns and cream at the end. Bring to the boil and remove from heat. Finish with a crescent of puff pastry or croûtons.

Mussel and Leek Soup

Partners 23, Sutton
Chef/proprietors Tim McEntire and Ian Thomason

5 pints (2.8 litres) mussels
12 oz. (350g.) potatoes, peeled and diced
butter
½ pint (275ml.) dry white wine
1½ lbs. (700g.) leeks, cleaned and chopped
2 pints (1.1 litres) fish stock
¼ pint (150ml.) cream
chives, chopped

Clean and wash the mussels discarding any that are open or damaged (see page 52).

Sweat the potatoes in a little butter without letting them colour. In a second pan bring the wine to the boil and plunge in the mussels in three or four batches. Cover with a lid and remove as soon as they open, discarding any that don't.

Add the leeks to the potatoes.

Remove the mussels from their shells and pass the cooking liquor through a fine sieve on to the leek and potato, reserving a little for later use. Add the fish stock and cook until the vegetables are soft. Purée them in a liquidiser and then pass through a coarse sieve. Reserve some of the mussels for the garnish, return the rest to the soup and liquidise again, just for a few seconds, which will be enough to shred the mussels without puréeing them.

Return the soup to a clean pan and add the cream. Season and correct consistency by adding a little extra mussel stock if necessary. Serve in warmed soup plates and garnish with the whole mussels and chopped chives.

Soupe de Poisson, Sauce Rouille

The Wife of Bath, Wye
Chef/proprietor Bob Johnson

Serves 6–8

fish heads and bones
9 fl. oz. (250ml.) white wine
9 fl. oz. (250ml.) water
2 onions
2 carrots
1 small head fennel
4 cloves garlic
olive oil
pinch of saffron
1 tablespoon Pernod
1 × 14 oz. (400g.) tin tomatoes
salt and freshly-ground pepper
croûtons, to serve

For the rouille sauce:

1 red chilli, seeded and chopped
2 cloves garlic, peeled
2 slices good, white bread, crusts removed
1 red pepper, seeds and pith removed
1 tablespoon paprika
olive oil
a little water
salt and freshly-ground black pepper

Boil the fish heads and bones with the wine and water for about 20–30 minutes to produce a good fish stock and strain off the liquid.

Peel and chop the onion, carrots, fennel and garlic and cook them in a little olive oil, stirring frequently.

Pound the saffron with a drop of Pernod, then add the fish stock. Add this, plus the tomatoes and the rest of the Pernod, to the vegetables and simmer until the vegetables are cooked. Pass through a Mouli, or liquidise in a blender and pass through a sieve. Return to the heat and add salt and freshly-ground black pepper to taste.

To make the rouille, blend all the sauce ingredients so that a fairly thick, smooth paste results. Serve separately with small croûtons.

Warm Prawn and Wild Garlic Salad

Lynwood House, Barnstaple
Chef Adam Roberts

5 wild garlic leaves per person
lettuce
watercress
radicchio
seasonal vegetables, finely sliced
bread for croûtons
a little grapeseed oil for cooking
prawns – as many as you want per person

For the dressing:

¼ pint (150ml.) raspberry vinegar
¾ pint (400ml.) grapeseed oil
salt

First collect your wild garlic leaves from either a river bank or a moist dark area; we collect ours from the banks of the River Taw in North Devon from mid February–June.

Make a salad by shredding the lettuce, watercress, radicchio and three of the wild garlic leaves per person, then add the vegetables. Put the dressing ingredients in a bottle, shake well to mix and pour over the salad.

In a little grapeseed oil evenly fry the croûtons and then set them aside. Turn the heat up high and add the prawns, tossing them quickly before throwing in, for a few moments, the remaining wild garlic leaves, coarsely chopped.

Arrange the salad on a warm plate with the croûtons and top with the prawns and wild garlic. Serve immediately.

Warm Skate Salad with Capers and Herb Dressing

Whites, Cricklade
Chef/proprietor Colin White

Serves 6

1½–2 lbs. (700–900g.) skate wings

For the dressing:

good virgin olive oil
white wine vinegar
salt
good selection of salad leaves
herbs: chervil, dill or fennel, chives, parsley etc., chopped
capers

Make a dressing with four parts oil to one part vinegar, then add the salt. If you can get really superb olive oil then don't spoil it with vinegar; if you like use a little lemon juice or maybe a touch of balsamic vinegar.

Steam or poach the skate wings for 10–15 minutes until they just flake easily at the thickest part. While they are cooking, add two-thirds of the herbs to the dressing. Prepare the salad leaves and toss with the dressing. Arrange on six plates.

Flake the hot fish from the bones and place on the salad. Scatter over the capers and the rest of the herbs and serve at once.

A Warm Salad of Smoked Salmon, Scallops, Asparagus and Green Leaves

Handsels, Edinburgh
Chef Andrew Radford

Serves 10

selection of green salad leaves; curly endive, chicory, watercress, sorrel, young spinach
1 oz. (25g.) mixed, roughly chopped parsley, chives and fennel
10 slices smoked salmon, cut into thin strips
20 scallops
walnut oil
20 asparagus tips, blanched and refreshed
salt and freshly-ground black pepper
1 cup brown bread croûtons, fried in walnut oil
half cup trimmed parsley
2 oz. (50g.) diced tomato

For the dressing:

2 fl. oz. (50ml.) walnut oil
2 fl. oz. (50ml.) peanut oil
2 fl. oz. (50ml.) white wine vinegar

Arrange the salad leaves on 10 large plates and sprinkle with half the chopped herbs and half the smoked salmon. Cut the scallops in two, discarding the black part and the grey-white gristle around the white cushion. Sauté the scallops in very hot walnut oil for 2–3 minutes until opaque and firm. Add the asparagus tips, the remaining herbs and smoked salmon. Season and sauté for a further minute.

Whisk together the oils and vinegar for the dressing and pour a little of it into the pan to deglaze. Divide the contents of the pan between the salad plates. Sprinkle with the croûtons, parsley and tomato. Warm the rest of the walnut dressing and serve it in a jug alongside the salad.

Marinated and Smoked Fish

Gravad Lax with Sweet Mustard Sauce

Pomegranates, London
Chef/proprietor Patrick Gwynn-Jones

Serves 20 as a starter

5 lbs. (2.3kg.) raw salmon, cut through bone
olive oil
good-sized bunch fresh dill
aquavit

For the pickling mixture:

1 breakfast cup sea salt
1½–2 cups granulated sugar
small handful white peppercorns, crushed
2 cloves, crushed

For the Lax sauce:

1 good-sized bunch of dill
1 lb. (450g.) white sugar
2 whole eggs
8 oz. (225g.) Dijon mustard
dash white wine vinegar
1 teaspoon salt
1 teaspoon black pepper
2 tablespoons Colman's English mustard powder
about 2 pints (1.1 litres) of oil

In the restaurant we, of course, use whole fish weighing up to 35lbs. each.

Mix all the ingredients for the pickling mixture together and put aside.

Scale but don't skin the fish, then fillet it and with tweezers extract every small bone. Take the two sides of salmon and smear with olive oil. Place the fish in a container on a bed of fresh dill and cover with a good layer of finely-chopped dill and about ½ inch (1cm.) layer of the pickling mixture. Over this sprinkle a small amount of aquavit. Place the other side of salmon, skin side up, on top, to complete the sandwich. Cover with more dill and place a weighted board on top.

The pickling time will vary with the thickness of the fish. My preference is for a maximum of 24 hours in a cool place (not the refrigerator). The whole fish must be turned over completely 2–3 times during the pickling process to enable both sides to be immersed equally in the juice.

To make the sauce, blend all the ingredients except the oil in a food processor. When smooth, add the oil slowly until a thick, creamy consistency is achieved.

To serve, lay one side down on a board, cover with chopped fresh dill and cut towards the tail in thick slices at a 45° angle. Serve with a small amount of sauce at the side and eat with caraway seed bread and a glass of iced aquavit.

Kilaw (Marinated fish with mango and a delicate coconut dressing)

Mansion House, Dartmouth
Chef/proprietor Richard Cranfield

Serves 8

2 lbs. (900g.) firm white fish fillets
lemon juice, to cover
2 medium onions, very finely sliced
salt
6 oz. (175g.) creamed coconut, grated
6 fl. oz. (175ml.) hot milk
1 clove garlic
1 teaspoon fresh root ginger, freshly grated
½ teaspoon ground black pepper
¼ teaspoon ground turmeric
1 mango, skinned and sliced
parsley or fresh coriander, finely chopped

Cover the fish with the lemon juice and add 1 teaspoon salt and the onions. Marinate in the refrigerator for 8 hours, stirring once or twice.

Blend the coconut with the milk, garlic, ginger, pepper and turmeric and cool. If the dressing seems too thick, add some more milk.

Drain and discard the lemon juice from the fish, then wash and pat the fish dry. Place the slices of mango on a plate and arrange the marinated fish on top. Spoon the dressing over and decorate with the parsley or coriander.

Marinated Grey Mullet

Corse Lawn House Hotel, Corse Lawn
Chef/proprietor Baba Hine

Serves 6

For the marinade:

2 oranges
4 limes
½ pint (275ml.) dry white wine
4 fl. oz. (125ml.) olive oil
small bunch chives, cut into 1 inch lengths
small bunch dill, very finely chopped
1 teaspoon soft green peppercorns
1 teaspoon sea salt
1 heaped tablespoon sugar

3 grey mullet

Peel the oranges and limes and cut the peel into julienne strips. Squeeze the juice from the fruit and place with all other ingredients for the marinade in a dish.

Fillet the mullet and remove all bones with a very sharp knife. Slice thinly (like smoked salmon), place the slices in the marinade and leave for six hours.

Remove from marinade and serve, garnished with strips of orange and lime peel from the marinade. This dish will keep in the refrigerator for two days.

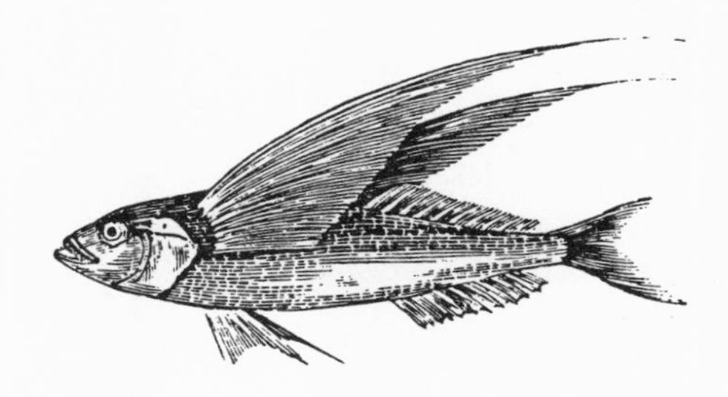

Watercress Pancakes with Creamed Arbroath Smokies

Homewood Park
Chef/proprietor Stephen Ross

Serves 6

For the watercress purée:

½ onion, finely chopped
2 oz. (50g.) butter
¼ pint (150ml.) cream
¼ pint (150ml.) milk
8–10 bunches of watercress, washed and any damaged or discoloured leaves discarded

For the pancake batter:

4 eggs
2 oz. (50g.) butter, melted
4 tablespoons flour

For the sauce:

3 Arbroath Smokie fillets
milk
¼ pint (150ml.) cream
freshly-grated nutmeg
freshly-ground black pepper

To make the watercress purée, sweat the onion in the butter and add the cream and milk. Bring to the boil and add the cress leaves. Cook for two minutes and then immediately liquidise.

Whisk together all the ingredients for the pancake mixture, making sure it is lump free, then add enough watercress purée to make a good batter.

Poach 3 Arbroath Smokie fillets in just enough milk to cover, for three minutes, then remove the flesh from the bones. Add the cream, nutmeg and pepper to the poaching liquor and then reduce it to a thick consistency. Return the fish to the pan.

Brush a heavy frying pan with a little butter, then make thin pancakes using 2–3 tablespoons of batter each time. Put a little of the fish filling on one half of each pancake. Fold them over and pour any surplus sauce around.

Arbroath Smokie Hotpots

White Moss House, Grasmere
Chef/proprietor Peter Dixon

Serves 4 as a starter

1 pair Arbroath Smokies, skinned, boiled and flaked
8 tablespoons double Jersey cream
fresh basil, dill or fennel, chopped
4 tomatoes, skinned, deseeded and chopped
freshly grated Parmesan cheese, or home-made dried breadcrumbs, fried with a little chopped garlic
twist of lemon or cucumber, or a sprig of parsley

This smokie recipe is very tasty and we think it worth the effort of finding real smokies rather than substituting other smoked fish. The use of fresh herbs greatly enhances this dish.

Season four large individual ramekin dishes and put in the fish. Add 2 tablespoons of cream and some chopped herbs to each dish. Divide the tomatoes between the four dishes and top with the Parmesan cheese or breadcrumbs. Heat in a medium oven for 20 minutes or grill until bubbling. Serve garnished with the lemon, cucumber or parsley.

Croustade of Arbroath Smokies

Thackeray's House, Tunbridge Wells
Chef/proprietor Bruce Wass

Serves 4 as a starter

1 pair Arbroath Smokies
½ pint (275ml.) fish stock
¼ pint (150ml.) milk
2½ oz. (60g.) butter
½ oz. (10g.) flour
¼ pint (150ml.) double cream
4 puff pastry cases
1 tomato, skinned, deseeded and diced
2 tablespoons chopped chives
lemon juice

Extract all the flesh from the smokies, keeping the skin and bones.

Simmer the skin and bones in the fish stock for twenty minutes before adding the milk. Bring to the boil then strain. Reduce the liquor by half. Blend together ½ oz. (10g.) of the butter and the flour and whisk it into the sauce. Add the cream and cook until smooth, stirring all the time.

Warm the smokie meat in the oven along with the pastry cases.

Whisk the remaining butter into the sauce followed by the tomato and chives with a few drops of lemon juice.

Place the pastry cases on a plate and fill them with hot smokie meat. Pour the sauce over and around it and serve.

Pasta Shells with Smoked Sea Trout and Vodka

Bridgefield House, Spark Bridge
Chef/proprietor Rosemary Glister

Serves 5–6 as a starter

4 oz. (125g.) pasta shells
4 oz. (125g.) smoked sea trout, cut into fine strips (smoked salmon is a good alternative)
small bunch of parsley, chopped
6 stuffed olives or black olives, chopped
2½ fl. oz. (60ml.) double cream
1 tablespoon Polish vodka
freshly-ground black pepper

Tip the pasta shells into a large pan of boiling, salted water and cook for 8–10 minutes until al dente. Drain and return to the pan.

Add the smoked sea trout and all the other ingredients. Stir carefully until the pasta is evenly coated.

Serve at once in hot scallop shells or ramekins.

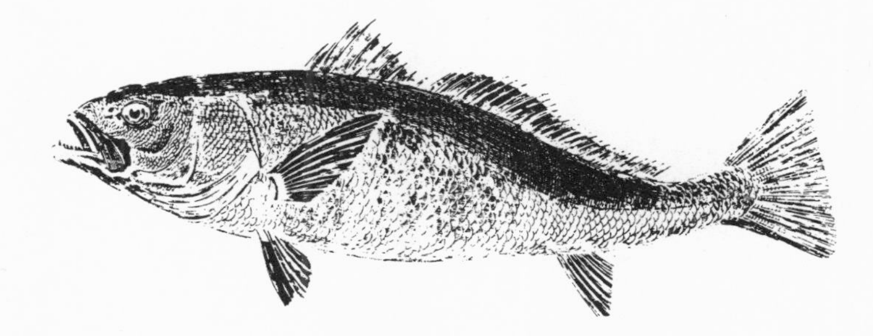

Terrines, Roulades and Soufflés

Hake and Laverbread Terrine with Fresh Crab Sauce

Grafton Manor, Bromsgrove
Chef Simon Morris

Serves 10–12

2 lbs. (900g.) hake fillets
1 egg
1 egg white
20 spinach leaves
1½ pints (900ml.) cream
salt and freshly-ground black pepper
6 teaspoons laverbread
chive flowers, to garnish

For the sauce:

2 live crabs
1 tablespoon chopped onion
1 tablespoon white wine
1 tablespoon double cream

Blend together the hake fillets, egg and egg white until the mixture resembles a purée. Chill for 1 hour.

Blanch the spinach leaves and use 15 to line a 4½ × 10 inch (11 × 25cm.) terrine.

Return the hake mixture to the blender and add the cream slowly, ensuring that it is well mixed. Add salt and pepper to taste and pass the mixture through a fine sieve into a chilled bowl.

Mix the hake mousse with the laverbread and place in the terrine. Cover with the remaining spinach leaves, tucking in the edges to seal completely, and tap the terrine gently to expel any air bubbles. Place in a bain-marie and cook for 55 minutes at 400F/200C/Gas 6.

To make the sauce, boil the live crabs for 10 minutes, cool and extract all the soft, creamy pink and yellow-brownish meat together with the white flesh from the body and claws. Discard the stomach, mouth and any white membranes or gills. Wash the shells thoroughly, then boil in about ½ pint (275ml.) water for 15–20 minutes to make stock. Sweat the onion and add the crab meat, white wine and 3 tablespoons of crab stock. Reduce by half and finish with a dash of double cream. Pour the crab sauce on to a warmed serving plate, place the terrine in the centre and garnish with the chive flowers.

Terrine of Sea Trout and Sole

Pool Court, Pool in Wharfedale
Chef Melvin Jordan

Serves 4–6

- 1 lb. (450g.) sea trout fillet, boned and skinned
- butter, for greasing
- salt and freshly-ground white pepper
- cayenne pepper
- freshly-grated nutmeg
- 12 fl. oz. (350ml.) double cream
- 8 oz. (225g.) lemon sole fillets, boned and skinned
- 4 oz. (125g.) leaf spinach, washed, blanched and liquidised

Place 8 oz. (225g.) of the sea trout between some thick plastic film and beat out gently until it is approximately ¼ inch (0.5cm.) thick. Lightly butter a terrine mould, approximately 6 inches (15cm.) long, 4 inches (10cm.) wide, 3 inches (7.5cm.) high. Sprinkle with a little salt, the peppers and some nutmeg, and then line the base and sides of the tin with the fish. Flatten a further 4 oz. (125g.) of the sea trout which will form the lid of the terrine. Leave in the refrigerator.

Liquidise the remaining sea trout and add 4 fl. oz. (125ml.) of cream. Blend until smooth but do not over-liquidise or it could curdle. Remove from the liquidiser and add salt and pepper to taste.

Liquidise the lemon sole and add the remaining cream. Blend until smooth. Divide the mixture in two, add the spinach purée to one half and season both.

Each of the three mousses must be kept cool at all times. If they become too warm they are liable to separate.

Form three alternate layers in the terrine and top with the sea trout lid. Cover with a buttered terrine lid or tin foil.

Cook in a bain-marie for 50 minutes at about 375F/190C/Gas mark 5. When it is cooked it will be just firm to the touch. Remove from the bain-marie and allow to cool before placing in the refrigerator to chill.

For the vinaigrette:

1 teaspoon Dijon mustard
2 tablespoons white wine vinegar
juice of 1 lemon
½ teaspoon Tabasco sauce
1 teaspoon soya sauce
¼ pint (150ml.) sunflower oil
approximately ¼ pint (150ml.) water
salt and freshly-ground black pepper

For the avocado dressing:

1 ripe avocado
¼ pint (150ml.) vinaigrette (see above)
2 fl. oz. (50ml.) water
juice of half a lemon

Make the vinaigrette by blending together mustard, vinegar, lemon juice, Tabasco and soya sauce. Gradually whisk in the oil. If the dressing seems too thick or strong, dilute with a little water, then add salt and pepper to taste. (The dressing can be kept up to 1 month in a screw-top jar in the refrigerator). To make the avocado dressing, peel, stone and mash the avocado, then blend with the remaining ingredients.

Serve the terrine cut into slices accompanied with the avocado dressing.

Galantine of Chew Valley Lake or Pink Trout

Hunstrete House, Chelwood
Chef Robert Elsmore

Serves 6

butter
1 oz. (25g.) onion, diced
7 trout fillets, skinned, approx. 3 oz. each, plus 4 oz. (125g.) extra, also skinned
1 oz. (25g.) fresh white bread (thin, no crust)
½ small egg white
1–2 tablespoons single cream
salt and freshly-ground black pepper
freshly-grated nutmeg
dash of English mustard powder
4 fl. oz. (125ml.) double cream, whipped
1 heaped teaspoon fresh dill, chopped
fish stock

Melt 1 tablespoon of butter, add the onion and cook without colouring, then leave to cool. Place the 4 oz. (125g.) trout fillets on a dish with the onion and bread. Moisten the fish with the egg white, add the single cream and sprinkle on salt, freshly-ground black pepper, nutmeg and a dash of mustard powder. Cover and chill.

Place the ingredients in a food processor, mix well and pass through a sieve. Place in a bowl, on ice, and gradually beat in the whipped cream and dill.

Place the remaining trout fillets between two sheets of polythene and lightly flatten them with a cutlet bat or rolling pin. Season the fillets with salt, pepper, nutmeg and a little mustard powder and lay flat on a large sheet of buttered foil, ensuring that all the fillets are side by side with the edges slightly overlapping. Fill any gaps with odd trimmings of the fillets. Pipe the trout forcemeat on to the fillets, covering them completely. Roll the mixture up as you would a Swiss roll, using the foil and twisting at each end. Chill for 2–3 hours, then unwrap gently and re-roll the sausage, this time using a clean, old tea-towel. Tie the ends securely. Place the whole thing in a pot or deep-sided tray of fish stock to cover and simmer for 30 minutes. Cool in the stock and when cold, chill in the refrigerator.

For the grape sauce:

juice of 3 lemons or limes
2 tablespoons caster sugar
5 tablespoons gin
1½lbs. (700g.) grapes, skinned
1 tablespoon arrowroot

To make the sauce, place the lemon or lime juice, sugar and gin in a pan and reduce. Add the grapes and cook for 2 minutes so that the grapes are just lightly cooked. Remove the grapes and place in a clean bowl. Add arrowroot to the liquor just to thicken. Sieve the juice over the grapes and leave to cool.

Remove the galantine from the refrigerator and unwrap. Cut into thin slices and arrange on a plate with a garnish of assorted lettuces tossed in vinaigrette, lemon wedges and the grape sauce.

Terrine of Salmon and Asparagus

Restaurant Nineteen, Bradford
Chef/proprietor Stephen Smith

Serves 14

1½lbs. (700g.) salmon
2 pints (1.1 litres) fish stock
2 medium carrots, finely chopped
1 medium onion, finely chopped
2 sticks celery, finely chopped
butter
¼ pint (150ml.) dry white wine
sprig of parsley
1 clove garlic, peeled
1 bay leaf
5 tomatoes, chopped
4 peppercorns
1 dessertspoon tomato purée
3 eggs, separated
¾ pint (400ml.) double cream
3 leaves gelatine, softened in a little water
juice of 1 small lemon
oil for greasing
1 lb. (450g.) asparagus, cooked, plus extra to serve

Bone the salmon, reserving the skin and bones. Gently poach the fish in the fish stock with a little salt for about 10–12 minutes. Remove and allow to cool. Reserve the stock.

Sauté the vegetables in a small knob of butter and add the salmon skins and bones to the pan. Ask your fishmonger for extra salmon bones if possible. Pour in the white wine and reduce. Stir and add the fish stock, parsley, garlic, bay leaf, tomatoes, peppercorns and tomato purée. Bring to the boil and simmer for ½ hour.

Strain and reduce the liquid over a high heat to about ½ pint (275ml.). Whisk the egg yolks and pour in the reduced stock. Bring 7 fl. oz. (200ml.) of the cream to the boil and add to the mixture. Gently thicken over a low heat, stirring continuously, and add the softened gelatine. Dissolve and allow to cool and then add the flaked salmon and lemon juice. As the mixture begins to set, fold in the remaining lightly-whipped cream and the whisked egg whites.

Lightly oil a loaf tin or terrine dish. Pour in a third of the mixture and run two or three lines of asparagus down the terrine. The mixture should be fairly thick when pouring into the terrine so that the asparagus will not sink. Repeat the process twice. Allow to set in the refrigerator. Unmould by dipping the terrine very briefly into hot water and turn out on to a tray. Serve with asparagus spears in a lemon dressing and Melba toast.

Smoked Haddock and Spinach Boudin with Apple

Partners 23, Sutton
Chef/proprietors Tim McEntire and Ian Thomason

Serves 6

8 oz. (225g.) smoked haddock fillet
2 oz. (50g.) egg white
6 fl. oz. (175ml.) double cream
10 oz. (275g.) spinach
white pepper
fish stock
walnut and peanut oils
lemon juice
3 crisp eating apples

Remove the large bones from the fish and purée in a food processor. Add the egg whites and work to a smooth paste. Push the mixture through a sieve twice and then refrigerate.

When the mixture is very cold, incorporate 2 fl. oz. (50ml.) of chilled cream and return to the refrigerator.

Wash the spinach well and blanch 4 oz. (125g.) of the largest leaves in boiling salted water.

Blend another 2 fl. oz. (50ml.) of cream into the fish and repeat the process after another half hour of refrigeration. Season with a pinch of white pepper and test for seasoning and consistency by poaching a coffee spoonful in gently simmering water. If the mousse is very firm, add a little more cream.

Drain the blanched spinach well and pat dry with a towel.

Using a large square of cling film, lay the spinach leaves best side down in a single band along the front edge, approximately 4 inches (10cm.) wide. Pipe the mousse on to the spinach and roll up the mixture in the cling film into a sausage shape, twisting the end to produce a cylinder. Poach in fish stock for 15 minutes and allow to cool.

When cold, slice and present on a bed of the remaining raw spinach, dressed with the nut oils and lemon juice. Garnish with fine strips of raw apple.

Pâté Barbue

L'Ortolan, Shinfield
Chef/proprietor John Burton-Race

Serves 16

1 lb. 2 oz. (500g.) brill, skinned, trimmed and boned
salt and freshly-ground white pepper
3 eggs
19 fl. oz. (525ml.) whipping cream
Pernod
lemon juice
6 oz. (175g.) unsalted butter, softened
tarragon, chervil and parsley, chopped very finely

For the crêpes:

9 fl. oz. (250ml.) milk
2 egg yolks
1 whole egg
1 oz. (25g.) melted butter
salt
2 oz. (50g.) flour

Make the pancakes in advance in the usual way.

Cut the brill into small pieces, put into a food processor and blend until very smooth. When this is finished the mixture may be a little warm so place in the refrigerator until cold. Return the mixture to the processor, add 1 teaspoon of salt and blend for another minute. Add the eggs one at a time, making sure they are well mixed.

Gradually add the cream to the mixture, making sure you scrape any brill from the sides of the processor bowl, until it is smooth and evenly mixed. Add a dash of Pernod, salt and ground white pepper and the juice of ¼ lemon. Remove the mixture from the processor and chill for 10 minutes.

Remove the mixture from the refrigerator and pass firmly but carefully through a fine chinois or very fine sieve. Add the butter all at the same time, beating very vigorously for about 20 seconds, making sure that it is well mixed but not overbeaten. This stage is very important because if you beat it too much the butter will split from the mixture.

Divide the mixture into two and add the herbs to one half.

Line a terrine mould with one layer of crêpes, all the way round without overlapping. Put one half of the white mixture in the bottom of the mould, spreading with a spatula, making sure to leave no holes or gaps. Then spread the herb mixture on top and finish with the other half of the white mixture.

Fold the crêpes over the top quite tightly, then put another two layers of crêpes on top, folding in neatly at the sides. Cover with a double layer of tin foil.

Place in a bain-marie of very hot, but not boiling, water. The water should be just below boiling point and the level about three-quarters of the way up the terrine. Cook in the oven at 300F/150C/Gas 2 for about 1½ hours. When firm to the touch, remove from the bain-marie and place on ice.

Cervelas of Salmon, Sole and Prawns on a Bed of Creamed Leeks

Mansion House, Dartmouth
Chef/proprietor Richard Cranfield

Makes about 14 sausages

1 lb. 1 oz. (475g.) salmon, boned and skinned
2 egg whites
2 pints (1.1 litres) double cream
2 teaspoons salt
8 oz. (225g.) sole fillet
11 oz. (300g.) butter
6 oz. (175g.) cooked prawns, peeled
1 tablespoon brandy
½ oz. (10g.) chives, snipped
½ oz. (10g.) green peppercorns
approx. 4 feet (1.22m.) pork sausage skins from the butcher
salt
5 oz. (150g.) breadcrumbs
14 oz. (400g.) leeks, washed, trimmed and finely sliced.

The poached sausages can be kept in their skins for a week in the refrigerator or can be frozen in their skins for later use.

To make the salmon mousse, put 15 oz. (425g.) of the salmon and the egg whites into a food processor and process for several minutes. Rub through a fine sieve into a bowl. Place the bowl in crushed ice. Using a wooden spoon, stir in 1 pint (570ml.) cream and 1 teaspoon salt, a little at a time and keep in a cool place.

Cut the fillet of sole and the remaining salmon into ¼ inch (0.5cm.) dice. Heat 1 tablespoon butter in a shallow pan and quickly sear the fish, a little at a time. Cool. Roll the prawns in 1 tablespoon of melted butter, pour in the brandy, ignite and cool. Pound the chives and green peppercorns in a bowl and add to the prawns. Stir all the ingredients into the salmon mousse.

Place the salmon mixture in a large piping bag with a big nozzle. Pull the sausage skin over the nozzle and tie a knot at the end of the skin. Gently pipe the salmon mixture into the skin, pricking with a pin to exclude any air pockets. When the sausage skin is full, tie up the end with string. Divide the sausage into 14 equal links, tying with kitchen string. Chill for 3 hours. Prick the sausages with a pin to prevent them from bursting during cooking. Poach the sausages gently in salted water for 15 minutes. Pour out the hot water and plunge the sausages into very cold water.

Preheat the oven to 225F/110C/Gas ¼. Using the point of a small, sharp knife, carefully cut off the sausage skin. Melt 2 oz. (50g.) butter and roll the sausages first in the butter and then in the breadcrumbs. Put the sausages in a sauté pan with 2 oz. (50g.) butter and sauté gently for 2 minutes. Place in the preheated oven for 7 minutes. Turn the sausages half-way through the cooking time.

Sweat the leeks in a shallow pan with the remaining butter until tender but crisp. Add a pint (570ml.) of cream, simmer gently to reduce to a creamy consistency and season to taste with salt.

Spread the leeks on a plate and arrange the sausages on top, having removed them very gently from the pan.

Salmon Strudel Perfumed with Basil

Crowthers Restaurant, East Sheen
Chef/proprietor Andrew Eastick

Serves 4

4 sheets filo pastry
2½ oz. (60g.) melted butter
1 lb. (450g.) fresh salmon
4 sprigs fresh basil, roughly chopped, plus extra to garnish
sea salt
2 fl. oz. (50ml.) Noilly Prat or dry sherry

For the sauce:

4 oz. (125g.) shallots, finely chopped
juice of one lime
4 fl. oz. (125ml.) dry white wine
pinch sugar
double cream (optional)
4 oz. (125g.) unsalted butter, softened
salt and cayenne pepper

Brush each sheet of filo pastry lightly with melted butter, then fold in half lengthwise and lay flat. Brush again with a little more butter.

Slice the salmon to a thickness of about ¼ inch (0.5cm.) as if carving smoked salmon. Lay the slices on the pastry in a single layer, scatter the basil leaves over the salmon and sprinkle with Noilly Prat and a little sea salt.

Roll up carefully, as for a Swiss roll, place on a greased baking sheet and brush with the remaining melted butter. Bake in a hot oven 400F/200C/Gas 6 for 6–8 minutes until golden brown.

To make the sauce, place the shallots, lime juice, white wine and sugar in a small saucepan. Bring to the boil and simmer to reduce by two-thirds. Remove from heat, cool slightly and add a little cream if desired.

Whisk in the softened butter, a little piece at a time, to thicken the sauce. Take care not to overheat at this stage. Season with salt and cayenne pepper.

To serve, flood 4 warm plates with the sauce and lay the sliced strudel on top. Garnish with sprigs of basil.

Hot Salmon Mousse on Smoked Salmon with Saffron Sauce

Wolfscastle Country Hotel, Haverfordwest
Chef Michael Lewis

Serves 6

6 slices good quality smoked salmon
watercress leaves

For the mousse:

8 oz. (225g.) fresh salmon fillet
1 egg white
½ pint (275ml.) double cream
salt
butter, for greasing
watercress, to garnish

For the sauce:

½ pint (275ml.) good fish stock
½ pint (275ml.) double cream
½ teaspoon saffron strands
salt and freshly-ground black pepper
2 teaspoons lemon juice

To prepare the mousse, blend the salmon fillet with the egg white and cream in a food processor until smooth. Rub the mixture through a sieve into a basin and add salt to taste. Put the mousse into 6 lightly-buttered, individual moulds and place these in a bain-marie. Cook in a moderate oven for 15 minutes. Test the mousse by inserting a skewer – when it comes out clean, the mousse is ready.

To make the sauce, reduce the fish stock vigorously until about 4 tablespoons remain. Add the cream and saffron and simmer very gently for 10 minutes. Add salt, black pepper and the lemon juice.

Place a slice of smoked salmon on large individual plates and turn the hot mousse out on to it. Pour over the sauce and garnish with watercress leaves.

Warm Crab and Gurnard Mousse with a Chervil Butter Sauce

Calcot Manor, Tetbury
Chef Ramon Farthing

Serves 4 as a starter

1 lb. (450g.) gurnard fillets, skinned and boned
2 fl. oz. (50ml.) fish stock
1 medium cock crab, cooked
salt
½ egg white
¾–1 pint (400–570ml.) double cream
freshly-ground black pepper
cayenne pepper
butter, for greasing
an assortment of salad leaves; mâche, frizzy, green, rosso

Cut the gurnard fillets into small cubes. Gently melt down the fish stock and add to the fish when slightly cool. Blend the two together in a food processor until smooth. Pass through a fine sieve and leave to cool in the refrigerator in a stainless steel bowl.

Prepare the crab, being careful to remove all bone and shell (see page 23). Separate the white and brown meats and allow to cool in the refrigerator.

Place the bowl containing the fish mousse over a tray of ice. Add a generous pinch of salt and the egg white and beat until thick. Add the cream little by little, beating back to thickness each time. Keep adding the cream until the thickness has reduced. Stir in a good grinding of black pepper, a touch of cayenne, then test the mousse for consistency and seasoning by placing some in a small, buttered mould. Cover with tin foil and put in a small bain-marie in a moderate oven for 5–8 minutes. Adjust texture and seasoning if necessary, then fold in the brown crab meat and put into buttered and cling-filmed moulds.

Make sure the mousse is firmly pressed down, then, using a teaspoon, spoon out the centre making a ½ inch (1cm.) hole. Place the white crab meat in the hole and pack in tightly. Spread the removed mousse back over the top. Cover with tin foil and refrigerate before cooking in the same way as before.

For the sauce:

2 shallots, chopped
2 fl. oz. (50ml.) white wine
2 fl. oz. (50ml.) white wine vinegar
½ pint (275ml.) whipping cream
6 oz. (175g.) unsalted butter, chilled and cubed
20 chervil leaves

To make the sauce, lightly colour the shallots in a little butter, then pour over the white wine and vinegar. Reduce to the consistency of syrup, whisk in the cream and simmer gently. Continue to whisk at intervals. When it has reduced by one-third, begin to add the unsalted butter, about three cubes at a time and whisk into the sauce completely before adding the next batch. Strain the sauce and keep warm.

Prepare the salad leaves in a circular formation, giving colour and height variation. Place the cooked mousses in the middle of the salad leaves which have been lightly seasoned. Add the chervil leaves to the sauce and spoon it gently around the salad leaves and plate, with a final spoonful over the actual mousse. Serve immediately.

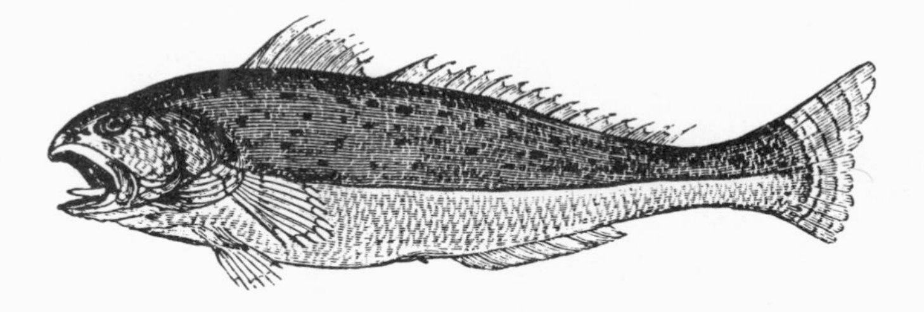

Smoked Eel and Pecan Nut Roulade

Bridgefield House, Spark Bridge
Chef/proprietor Rosemary Glister

Serves 6 as a starter – 2 thin slices each

For the roulade:

oil for greasing
2 eggs separated, plus 1 extra egg white
pinch of ground ginger
¼ teaspoon either onion or garlic salt
½ oz. (10g.) soft brown sugar
3 oz. (75g.) shelled pecan nuts, chopped very fine

For the filling:

4 oz. (125g.) smoked eel flesh without skin or bones (about one full small eel)
6 oz. (175g.) soft fat cheese
1 teaspoon horseradish sauce
2 tablespoons soured or double cream
freshly-ground sea salt and black pepper

To make the roulade, line a greased 10 × 8 inch (25 × 20cm), tin with oiled parchment paper. Beat the egg yolks and add the ginger, onion or garlic salt and sugar. Carry on whisking until thick. Whisk egg whites until stiff and fold in a third of the stiff egg whites into the yolk mixture. Whisk remaining egg whites again and fold into the mixture. Gently fold in the nuts. Gently turn out into the prepared tin and bake in a preheated oven at 350F/180C/Gas 4 for about 12–15 minutes. It is cooked when a skewer comes out cleanly. Leave to cool.

To make the filling, put the smoked eel flesh through a food processor or liquidiser. Add the remaining ingredients and beat until smooth. When the roulade is cool, turn out, spread with the eel mixture and roll up like a Swiss roll.

Serve in slices as a starter with a garnish of twisted lemon and cucumber, pipped black grapes and, if in season, sliced strawberries.

Crab Soufflé

Cleeveway House, Bishops Cleeve
Chef/proprietor John Marfell

Serves 4

4 oz. (125g.) butter
4 oz. (125g.) flour
½ pint (10 fl. oz.) milk
4 oz. (125g.) Cheddar cheese, grated
1 tablespoon medium dry sherry
1 tablespoon brandy
salt and freshly-ground black pepper
6 oz. (175g.) crab meat, white and brown
4 eggs, separated

Make a roux with the butter and flour, then gradually stir in the milk. Add the grated cheese, sherry and brandy and season with salt and pepper. Lastly add the crab meat, adjust the seasoning and stir until thick. Keep warm on the side of the stove.

Beat the egg whites until stiff but not dry. Fold 3 egg yolks into the crab mixture off the stove and then fold in the beaten egg whites. Place in ovenproof soup bowls or pots and cook in a very hot oven for 14 minutes.

Taken from 'The Restaurant Recipe Book'.

Hot Mousseline of Red Mullet with Sweet Basil Sauce

Teignworthy Hotel, Frenchbeer
Chef David Woolfall

Serves 4–5

For the mousseline:

14 oz. (400g.) red mullet, filleted and small bones removed
salt
cayenne pepper
butter for greasing
18 fl. oz. (500ml.) double cream, chilled

For the sauce:

2 tablespoons shallots, chopped
2½ fl. oz. (60ml.) dry white wine
½ pint (275ml.) chicken stock
12 fl. oz. (350ml.) double cream
1 good bunch sweet basil, a few leaves reserved to garnish
1 tablespoon spinach or watercress purée
salt and freshly-ground black pepper
small knob of butter

Chill the mullet fillets well, then purée in a blender. Transfer the flesh to a bowl set in iced water and season with salt and cayenne pepper. Gradually add the chilled cream, very slowly at first. When all the cream is incorporated, pass the mousseline through a fine sieve and set aside. Butter 4 or 5 ramekins and fill with the mousseline. Poach them in a bain-marie in the oven at 350–400F/180–200C/Gas 4–6 for 12–15 minutes.

To make the sauce, place the shallots and wine in a pan and reduce to a syrupy consistency. Add the chicken stock and reduce by half. Add the double cream and boil for two minutes, then add the basil and boil for a further minute. Add the spinach or watercress purée, then liquidise. Pass through a fine sieve. Test for seasoning, then whisk in the butter.

Pour the sauce on to individual plates and turn out the mousselines into the centre. Garnish with a few basil leaves.

Pike and Char Soufflé

White Moss House, Grasmere
Chef/proprietor Peter Dixon

Serves 6

3 oz. (75g.) pike
3 oz. (75g.) char (salmon may be substituted)
salt and freshly-ground black pepper
white wine
½ pint (275ml.) milk or milk and part fish stock made from the pike bones
2 oz. (50g.) butter, plus extra for greasing
2 oz. (50g.) plain flour
pinch of cayenne
pinch of nutmeg
4 egg yolks
3 oz. (75g.) grated cheese (Double Gloucester gives a rich colour to the soufflé)
1 tablespoon fennel, dill or basil, chopped
5 egg whites
pinch of cream of tartar

Pike from one of the lakes, such as Rydal Water, is often cleaner and has a less muddy flavour than river pike. Char is a delicate pink-fleshed fish, found in Windermere, Coniston, Crummock Water and some Scottish lochs; it is a deep water fish which is line-caught from boats. A special permit is needed and these are limited to protect numbers.

Lightly poach the fish with a little salt, black pepper and white wine to cover. Flake the fish when cooked (about 5 minutes). Bring the milk, or milk and stock, to the boil and keep on the stove at a simmer.

Melt the butter and stir in the flour with a wooden spoon. Cook until foaming but not brown for two minutes. Remove from the heat and when the bubbling stops, add boiling milk. Add ½ teaspoon salt, ¼ teaspoon black pepper, the cayenne and nutmeg and whisk vigorously. Return to the heat for 1 minute, whisking continuously. Remove from the heat and add the egg yolks one at a time. The mixture can be prepared up to this point beforehand, but bring back to a tepid temperature before proceeding.

Add the fish, cheese and herbs. Beat the egg whites until stiff with a pinch of salt and cream of tartar. Stir the initial spoonful into the mixture, then fold in the rest. Place in buttered ramekins; smooth and mark the top. Cook in a bain-marie for 5 minutes at 375F/190C/Gas 5, then 40 minutes at 350F/180C/Gas 4. Serve immediately.

Shellfish

Fresh Scallops in Cream Sauce

Lynwood House, Barnstaple
Chef/proprietor Ruth Roberts

Serves 2

10 nice plump fresh scallops
2 oz. (50g.) butter
sea salt and freshly-ground black pepper
1 fl. oz. (25ml.) brandy
4 fl. oz. (125ml.) white wine
¼ pint (150ml.) single or whipping cream
1 teaspoon of chopped, fresh tarragon or marjoram
1 tablespoon each finely sliced carrot, celery, onion, radish

This is a wonderful dish of contrasting colour and texture.

Ask your fishmonger to remove scallops from their shells. Cut out the black part and the grey, gristly pieces, then thoroughly wash them and dry them in a paper towel. Heat butter in a frying pan and, when sizzling, add the scallops, lightly season them with sea salt and freshly-milled pepper. Turn over after 25 seconds and cook them for a similar time. Flambé with the brandy. Add the white wine, cream and herbs, (do not use dried herbs as they are too harsh).

Remove the scallops to a serving dish. Reduce the sauce until it lightly coats the back of a wooden spoon which will take about two to three minutes. Whilst the sauce is reducing, plunge the finely chopped vegetables into seasoned boiling water for 10 seconds, then drain and strew them around the scallops. Pour the sauce over the scallops and serve.

Scallops Poached in Sweet White Wine and Basil

Thornbury Castle, Thornbury
Chef Colin Hingston

Serves 2

2 oz. (50g.) chopped celery, carrot and onion
butter
2 fl. oz. (50ml.) sweet white wine e.g. Sauternes
¼ pint (150ml.) strong fish stock
¼ pint (150ml.) cream
small bunch fresh basil, chopped
salt and freshly-ground black pepper
8 medium scallops

Sweat the vegetables in a small knob of butter. Add the wine and reduce by half. Add the fish stock and reduce it to a sticky fumet, i.e. very concentrated and slightly syrupy.

Add the cream and reduce to a fairly thick sauce. Strain out the vegetables, add the chopped basil and season to taste. Bring the sauce to the boil and add the trimmed, prepared scallops (see page 43).

Bring back to the boil and simmer for 30 seconds. Serve.

Hot Scallop Pudding

Thackeray's House, Tunbridge Wells
Chef/proprietor Bruce Wass

Serves 4 as a starter

4 oz. (125g.) unsalted butter, plus extra for greasing
6 large scallops (for preparation see page 43)
1 egg
¼ pint (150ml.) whipping cream
salt and freshly-ground black pepper
1 heaped tablespoon chopped fresh herbs
4 fl. oz. (125ml.) dry vermouth or dry white wine
½ pint (275ml.) fish stock
¼ pint (150ml.) double cream

Butter 4 dariole moulds and put them in the refrigerator to harden the butter.

Liquidise four scallops with the egg and whipping cream to form a mousse. Season.

Dice the other two scallops into 10 pieces each. Heat 1 oz. (25g.) of the butter in a frying pan and as it turns brown throw in the scallops and sauté for 30 seconds. Now cool them and mix in half the herbs.

Line the bottom and sides of the dariole moulds with the mousse. Place the diced scallops in the middle and then cover with more mousse. Seal the top with greased tin foil and cook in a medium oven for approximately 20–30 minutes or until the puddings are firm to the touch.

Meanwhile boil the vermouth or wine and fish stock, reducing it to a glaze. Add the double cream and boil, stirring continuously, until a nice light sauce is obtained.

When the puddings are cooked, turn out on to warm plates. If any liquid issues from the mousses, tip it into the sauce. Whisk the remaining butter and the rest of the herbs into the sauce and pour over the puddings.

Scallops in a Noilly Prat Sauce

Pool Court, Pool in Wharfedale
Chef Melvin Jordan

Serves 4

16 fresh king scallops
16 fl. oz. (450ml.) Noilly Prat vermouth
3 shallots, finely chopped
½ pint (275ml.) fish stock (made in the usual manner ensuring bay leaves, juniper berries and bouquet garni are included)
½ pint (275ml.) double cream
12 oz. (350g.) unsalted butter
lemon juice
freshly-milled salt and black pepper

Prise open the scallop shells retaining the natural juices for the marinade. Clean and prepare the scallops in the usual way (see page 43). Cut them in half and marinate for 30–40 minutes in the Noilly Prat, shallots and the scallop juices. Stir occasionally. Remove the scallops and then pour the marinade and the fish stock into a saucepan. Bring to the boil. Add the scallops and poach in this liquid for 2–3 minutes. Now lift them out and keep warm.

Reduce the stock and the Noilly Prat mixture almost to a glaze, (this will be dark caramel in colour). Whisk in the cream and bring it gently to the boil. Remove the sauce from the heat and whisk in the butter, a little at a time, until the sauce is light and airy. If necessary adjust the seasoning with a little lemon juice, salt and pepper and additional Noilly Prat. Place the scallops on a warm dish and coat with a little sauce, offering the remainder separately.

Crayfish, Scallop and Mussel Pastry with Basil Sauce

Handsels, Edinburgh
Chef Andrew Radford

Serves 10

hazelnut oil
40 scallops, cleaned and prepared (see page 43)
6 shallots, finely chopped
salt and black pepper
80 mussels, opened and shelled (see page 52)
40 crayfish, shelled and cleaned
80 × 8 inch (20.5cm.) square sheets filo pastry, about 4 lbs. (1.8kg.)
melted butter
4 oz. (125g.) finely chopped parsley
3 large sprigs basil
1 egg, beaten
½ pint (275ml.) white wine
¼ (150ml.) white wine vinegar
1 teaspoon saffron
½ pint (275ml.) double cream
8 oz. (225g.) unsalted butter, chilled and diced

Using a thick bottomed pan, heat a little hazelnut oil until very hot. Quickly seal the scallops with a third of the shallots and season. Turn out of the pan on to a piece of kitchen towel. Sauté, then pat dry the washed mussels and crayfish tails.

To prepare the pastry, take one 8 inch (20.5cm.) square sheet of filo and brush with melted butter. Continue until you have four sheets in all. Repeat this process to make 20 piles of 4 sheets. Keep the filo covered with a damp tea towel until brushed with the butter so that it does not dry out. On top of each pile place in the centre 2 crayfish, 2 scallops and 4 mussels. Sprinkle with a little parsley, salt and pepper and some of the finer basil leaves, chopped. Brush around the edge of the pastry squares with a little of the beaten egg, then pull the four corners of the pastry up and over the fish, to cover completely, and twist. Open out the corners to resemble petals. Continue to assemble the parcels and then brush all the pastries with the remaining egg. Place the parcels in the oven at 375F/190C/Gas 5 for 15 minutes until golden brown.

Meanwhile add the remaining shallots, white wine, white wine vinegar, saffron and basil to the pan you used earlier and reduce by half. Add the double cream and reduce further until it is thick and syrupy. Whisk in the butter pieces 2–3 at a time and allow the sauce to boil for approximately 30 seconds. Strain and keep warm. Pour a little of the basil butter sauce to the front of 10 warm plates, place two pastries in the middle of each plate and serve immediately.

Mussels in a Cream and Curry Sauce

Michael's, Bristol
Chef/proprietor Michael McGowan

Serves 6

8 pints (4.5 litres) fresh mussels, cleaned
½ pint (275ml.) dry white wine
½ pint (275ml.) water
2 onions, chopped

For the sauce:

2 oz. (50g.) butter
2 dessertspoons flour
2 dessertspoons curry powder
6–8 tablespoons double cream
salt and freshly-ground black pepper

This dish may be served as a starter or as a main course with rice.

Clean the mussels thoroughly, removing barnacles and beards. Make sure you discard all dead mussels. Cook the mussels in batches in the wine and water with the onions. As soon as they open, remove the mussels, add the next batch and so on until all are cooked. Discard any mussels that have not opened. Strain and reserve the liquid.

Make a roux with the butter, flour and curry powder. Gradually add 1 pint of the strained juices and bring to the boil. More of the cooking liquid may be added if the sauce is too thick. Add the cream and seasoning to taste. Add the mussels and heat through, then serve immediately.

Cockles and Mussels

Grafton Manor, Bromsgrove
Chef Nicola Morris

Serves 4–6

2 pints (about 1¼ lbs.) cockles
8 pints (or 8 lbs.) mussels
½ clove garlic
1 tablespoon mixed, freshly chopped chives, thyme and parsley, plus extra to garnish
½ medium onion, chopped
1 oz. (25g.) butter
¼ pint (150ml.) white wine
¼ pint (150ml.) fish stock
¼ pint (150ml.) double cream

Clean, debeard and debarnacle the cockles and mussels in several changes of cold water, throwing away any broken ones and any that do not close when sharply tapped.

In a large saucepan, sweat the onion, garlic and herbs in the butter until the onion is soft. Add the wine, fish stock and cream and bring to the boil. At this point, add the cockles and mussels and cook until the shells are open (about 4 minutes). Discard any unopened shells.

Serve immediately in large dishes, using all the pan juices and sprinkled with extra freshly chopped herbs.

Pêche de Homard et de Lotte et son Oeuf Poché, Sauce Américaine

The Bell Inn, Aston Clinton
Chef Kevin Cape

Serves 2

2¼ lbs. (1kg.) live lobster, to obtain: 7 oz. (200g.) lobster, 1 tail, 2 claws
6 oz. (175g.) monkfish, cut into 8 equal pieces
fish stock
2 eggs
2 egg yolks
2 dessertspoons white wine
7 fl. oz. (200ml.) double cream, lightly whipped
½ oz. (10g.) chopped herbs
½ tomato, skinned, deseeded and diced
few thin strips of vegetables
butter
sprigs of chervil

To make 18 fl. oz. (500ml.) of sauce, crush the shells and put them into a hot pan. Fry for several minutes, then add the brandy and flambé. Add the mirepoix of vegetables, garlic, thyme, bay leaf and tomato purée and cook gently for several minutes. Add the fish stock and bring to the boil. Allow to simmer gently for 20 minutes.

Mix the butter and flour together to form a paste and whisk into the sauce. Bring back to the boil and continue cooking for another 20 minutes. Add salt and pepper, then pass through a fine sieve. Add a little fish stock if the sauce is too thick. Use half this quantity and freeze the rest in an airtight container.

Place the live lobster in a pan of boiling salted water, bring back to the boil and cook for 5 minutes. Remove the pan from the heat and allow the lobster to cool in the cooking liquor. When cold, remove the meat from the shell, first discarding the stomach and the black intestine. Cut the tail into four pieces, leaving the claws whole.

Season the monkfish and poach gently in fish stock. When three-quarters cooked, remove the fish and allow to cool.

For the sauce:

5 oz. (150g.) lobster shells
a splash of brandy
mirepoix of 2 oz. (50g.) onion, 1 oz. (25g.) carrot, 1 oz. (25g.) celery
1 clove garlic, diced
sprig of thyme
small bay leaf
1 oz. (25g.) tomato purée
18 fl. oz. (500ml.) fish stock
1 oz. (25g.) butter
1 oz. (25g.) flour
salt and freshly-ground black pepper

Poach two eggs in a pan of simmering water. Make an egg sabayon by placing two egg yolks in a small bowl; add the white wine and whisk over a bowl of warm water until the mixture thickens and a trail is left when the whisk is removed and passed over the mixture. To this add the cream, herbs, tomato, sauce Américaine and some seasoning; fold together.

Cook the vegetable strips in a little butter. Place the lobster, monkfish and poached eggs in some fish stock to re-heat for 3–4 minutes; this will also finish cooking the fish. Place the vegetables in the centre of the plate and put the pieces of lobster and monkfish alternately around the vegetables. Place the poached eggs on top and coat with the sauce. Wipe the edges of the plates to remove any drips and glaze under a hot grill until golden brown all over. Garnish with the lobster claws and sprigs of chervil.

Moules Marinières with Garlic

Wolfscastle Country Hotel, Haverfordwest
Chef Michael Lewis

Serves 4

4 dozen mussels
butter
4 shallots, skinned and finely chopped
6 cloves of garlic, peeled and crushed
½ bottle dry white wine
chopped parsley
2 sprigs of thyme
1 bay leaf
freshly-ground black pepper
2 level teaspoons flour
salt (optional)

Put the mussels in a large bowl under running water. Scrape off the mud, barnacles and beards with a sharp knife. Discard any that are open or cracked. Rinse again until there is no trace of sand in the bowl.

Melt a large knob of butter and sauté the shallots until soft. Add the garlic, wine, a small handful of chopped parsley, the thyme, bay leaf and several turns of the peppermill. Cover and simmer for 10 minutes. Add the drained mussels, cover and steam, shaking often, until the shells open; this will take about 5 minutes. Holding the mussels over the saucepan to catch the juices, remove the top shells and place the mussels in warm soup plates.

Keep the mussels warm while you strain the liquor and reduce it by half. Cream a small knob of soft butter with the flour and add this, a small piece at a time, to the sauce to thicken it. Adjust the seasoning, adding salt if needed. When the sauce is cooked, pour it over the mussels, sprinkle with extra chopped parsley and serve immediately.

Gratin de Belons

Provence at the Gordleton Mill, Lymington
Chef/proprietor Jean-Pierre Novi

Serves 6

36 Belons (Whitstables or other oysters may be substituted)
2 leeks, finely sliced
4 fl. oz. (125ml.) Noilly Prat
4 fl. oz. (125ml.) double cream
butter
salt and freshly-ground black pepper
1 egg yolk

Open the belons with an oyster knife. Remove the oysters from their shells, reserving both the shells and the oyster juices. Blanch the leeks for 1 minute and leave to cool. Boil the Noilly Prat and the oyster liquor. Poach the belons in this liquid for 30 seconds and then remove them. Continue to boil the liquid until reduced by half. Add the cream and keep the sauce warm.

Warm the leek slices with a little melted butter, salt and pepper. Place the cleaned shells on an oven tray with some slices of leek in each. Put the oysters on the bed of leek. The shells can be kept upright by putting them on a bed of coarse sea salt.

Whisk the egg yolk with a little water and mix it into the sauce off the heat. Pour the sauce over each oyster and place the tray under a very hot grill for 30 seconds. Place six oysters on each plate and serve immediately.

Oysters Baked on Puréed Leeks with a Champagne and Caviar Sauce

Flitwick Manor, Flitwick
Chef Geoffrey Welch

Serves 2

6 Native oysters (No. 2's) per person
6 dessertspoons leek purée per person
butter
coarse sea salt
freshly snipped chives, to garnish

For the champagne sauce:

juices reserved from opening oysters
3 tablespoons dry champagne
1 shallot, very finely chopped
2 tablespoons double cream
2 oz. (50g.) unsalted butter, diced
½ oz. (10g.) caviar or lumpfish roe (black)

To make the sauce, place the oyster juices, champagne and chopped shallots in a small saucepan. Boil and reduce until about 1 tablespoon of liquid remains. Add the double cream. Boil until the sauce begins to thicken, reduce the heat to very low, then whisk in the diced butter. Remove from heat. Keep warm until needed and mix in the caviar at the last moment.

Open the oysters and remove them carefully from their shells with a teaspoon, having first cut through the muscle that attaches them with a sharp knife. These operations should be carried out over a strainer held over a small saucepan to catch the juices. Reserve the hollow halves of the shells. Put the oysters into iced water for 20–30 seconds to firm them up. Place them on absorbent kitchen paper to dry.

Warm the leek purée in a little butter and place a dessert-spoonful in each half shell with an oyster on each. Cover a dinner plate or gratin dish with sea-salt and place the oyster shells on top. Bake in a hot oven for 3–4 minutes. Cover the oysters with the champagne and caviar sauce and sprinkle the chives on top.

Prawns in a Case with Avocado Sauce

Danescombe Valley Hotel, Danescombe Valley
Chef/proprietor Anna Smith

Serves 6 as a starter

2 oz. (50g.) butter, slightly softened
eighth teaspoon ground mace
1–2 tablespoons tomato juice
dash Tabasco sauce
1 lb. (450g.) fresh prawns
1 lb. (450g.) puff pastry
salt and freshly-ground black pepper
1 ripe avocado
juice of a lime

Cream the butter with the mace until soft, beat in the tomato juice and Tabasco and place in a shallow flameproof casserole. Strew the prawns on top of the butter, cover the dish and set aside.

Roll out the pastry, not too thinly, and cut out small rounds. Bake them in a hot oven for 10–15 minutes until well risen and crisp.

Place the prawns and butter mixture over a gentle heat, just enough to melt the butter. Sprinkle over a little salt and black pepper, then rotate the pan so that the prawns are well coated and impregnated with the spices and seasoning.

Place the avocado flesh with the lime juice, salt and pepper in a liquidiser and blend until smooth.

Split the rounds of pastry and fill with the prawns. Serve surrounded by the avocado sauce with a green salad or fresh asparagus.

Dublin Bay Prawns Stir Fried with Cashew Nuts

Kirkby Fleetham Hall, Kirkby Fleetham
Chef Ray Sharp

Serves 4

24 Dublin Bay prawns, peeled
salt
cayenne pepper
1 tablespoon vegetable oil
4 oz. (125g.) cashew nuts, unsalted
2 oz. (50g.) redcurrant jelly
2 fl. oz. (50ml.) white wine vinegar
4 oz. (125g.) tinned tomatoes, chopped
½ pint (275ml.) fish stock
4 fl. oz. (125ml.) natural yoghurt
4 oz. (125g.) long grain rice, cooked
4 oz. (125g.) wild rice, cooked

Season the Dublin Bay prawns with salt and cayenne pepper. Heat the oil in a large frying pan or wok and toss the prawns in the hot oil. Drain and keep warm. Now add the cashew nuts, redcurrant jelly and vinegar to the pan. Cook for one minute before augmenting the sauce with the tomatoes and fish stock. Simmer for two minutes or until the jelly has completely dissolved.

Return the Dublin Bay prawns to the pan and boil for one minute. Add a swirl of natural yoghurt and serve surrounded by a piping hot border of long grain and wild rice.

Fresh Prawns Cooked in a Cream and White Wine Sauce with Tarragon and Vegetables

Sharrow Bay Hotel, Ullswater
Chefs Juan Martin and Colin Akrigg and the Team of Six

Serves 6

30 Dublin Bay prawns
about 1 pint (570ml.) court bouillon
butter, or lobster butter, for cooking
anchovy essence (optional)

For the sauce:

2 young carrots
2 sticks celery
2 shallots
2 young leeks
½ pint (275ml.) white wine
¼ pint (150ml.) tarragon vinegar
1 oz. (25g.) tarragon, finely chopped
lemon juice
¾ pint (400ml.) double cream
salt and black pepper
butter or lobster butter

To make the sauce, slice all the vegetables finely and cook in the white wine and vinegar, adding a little water if required. Strain the vegetables and add the tarragon and lemon juice. Keep warm.

Reduce the liquid by half and add the cream. Reduce to the desired consistency and add salt and pepper. Pass through a fine strainer on to the vegetables and tarragon. Check the seasoning, adding some butter or lobster butter if required.

Cook the prawns in a court bouillon for about three minutes. Remove the tails and shells. Toss in butter or lobster butter for a few minutes. Add the sauce and a little anchovy essence if liked, and serve in a small copper pot.

Fricassée of Prawns and Sweetbread in a Puff Pastry Case

Longueville House, Mallow
Chef John Sheedy

Serves one

6 pieces of sweetbread
1½ × 3 inch (3.5 × 7.5cm.) piece of puff pastry
beaten egg
6 prawns (shelled)
2 tablespoons very finely chopped leek
2 fl. oz. (50ml.) vegetable stock
1 fl. oz. (25ml.) cream
1 oz. (25g.) unsalted butter
salt and freshly-ground white pepper
basil

Blanch the sweetbreads and remove the membranes. Brush the puff pastry with a little beaten egg and cook in the oven at 400F/200C/Gas 6 for 12 minutes together with the prawns which should be placed in a hot, non-stick pan. Cook the leek in a little butter and water.

Remove the prawns and puff pastry from the oven. Place the puff pastry on a plate, slice it in two and place the leek in the centre with the prawns on top.

De-glaze the prawn pan with the vegetable stock. Reduce the stock and add the cream, butter and seasoning. Put some sweetbread on the side of the plate. Add some basil to the sauce and pour it around the pastry.

Gambas Wrapped in Filo Pastry with Baby Leeks, Beansprouts and Green Chillies

Woods, Bath
Chef Mary Alley

Serves 4

2 baby leeks, finely sliced
1 large clove garlic, crushed
2 spring onions, finely sliced
1 green chilli, finely chopped
sesame oil
6 fl. oz. (175ml.) soy sauce
3 fl. oz. (75ml.) dry sherry
2 teaspoons clear honey
1 large handful beansprouts
4 sheets filo pastry
3 fl. oz. (75ml.) melted butter or oil
8 large Gambas, peeled but with the tail left on

For the sauce:

7 fl. oz. (200ml.) Natural Greek homemade yoghurt
1 dessertspoon toasted sesame seeds
½ teaspoon crushed garlic
1 teaspoon Dijon mustard
½ teaspoon lemon juice

Fry the leeks with the garlic, spring onion and chilli in a little oil (preferably sesame oil). Add the soy sauce, sherry and honey, then add the beansprouts and cook until they are just softened.

Use the melted butter to brush the four sheets of filo pastry, cut each in half lengthways and lay one gamba across each piece of pastry. Drain the vegetable mixture and add one spoonful to each portion. Fold over one side, leaving the other side with the tail exposed. Then roll up tightly and brush with melted butter. Bake in a preheated oven at 450F/230C/Gas 8 for about 8–10 minutes or until golden brown all over.

Mix together all the ingredients for the sauce and serve.

Sea and Fresh-water Fish

Seafood Platter

Fischer's, Baslow
Chef/proprietor Max Fischer

Serves 4

5 oz. (150g.) selection of prepared fish and shellfish per person (Dover Sole, Lemon Sole, Monkfish, fresh Salmon, Turbot, Scallops or King Prawns)

For the sauce:

2 medium-sized carrots, finely sliced
5 shallots, cut into julienne strips
7 fl. oz. (200ml.) water
bouquet garni (thyme, bay leaf, 3 cloves, parsley, pinch freshly-ground white pepper, pinch sugar)
4 oz. (125g.) unsalted butter, diced
white wine vinegar
cucumber, cut into julienne strips
tomato, skinned, deseeded and diced
garden herbs

To make the sauce, place the carrots, shallots, water and bouquet garni in a pan and bring to the boil. Simmer until the carrots are al dente.

Meanwhile lightly steam the fish and arrange on hot plates. Keep warm in the oven.

Whisk in the unsalted butter a little at a time to thicken the sauce. Reduce slightly, season and add a little white wine vinegar. Finally add the cucumber and tomato to the sauce before spooning over the fish and decorating with sprigs of fresh garden herbs.

Serve the platter with new potatoes and a side salad.

Filets de Poisson à La Florentine

The Wife of Bath, Wye
Chef/proprietor Bob Johnson

Serves 6–8

For the sauce:

head and bones of the fish
9 fl. oz. (250ml.) white wine
9 fl. oz. (250ml.) water
2 oz. (50g.) butter
2 oz. (50g.) flour
8 oz. (225g.) grated Cheddar or other mild cheese, plus extra for garnishing
½ nutmeg, grated
1 chicken stock cube
½ pint (275ml.) double cream
salt and freshly-ground black pepper

1 lb. (450g.) fish, filleted
2 heads bulb fennel, finely sliced
1 lb. (450g.) leaf spinach, washed and trimmed
butter, for greasing and cooking

Any white fish will suffice, but particularly good are sole, turbot or brill. Your fishmonger will fillet the fish for you, but try to obtain the head and bones for stock.

To make the sauce, boil the fish heads and bones for about 20–25 minutes with the wine and water. Strain off liquid and retain.

Melt the butter, add the flour to make a roux, then gradually add the fish stock and bring to the boil, whisking to ensure a smooth sauce. Whisk in the cheese and nutmeg. Crumble the chicken stock cube, stir in and simmer, whisking every few minutes to prevent burning. Add the cream.

Poach the fennel in a little water until just tender – about 10 minutes. Add spinach for a further 5 minutes and strain well. Butter a shallow, ovenproof dish and arrange fennel and spinach in six small heaps.

Gently fry the fish fillets in butter for two minutes each side. Place a fillet (or two) on each of the fennel and spinach portions. Pour over the cheese sauce, lightly dust with grated cheese and cook in a fairly hot oven until browned on top (about 15 minutes).

Fillets of Prime Fish en Papillote

Whites, Cricklade
Chef/proprietor Colin White

Serves 6

2½ lbs. (1.1kg.) prime fish fillets
1 small carrot
1 or 2 inside sticks celery
¼ head of bulb fennel
2 small leeks
6 circles buttered greaseproof paper 16–18 inches (40–45cm.)
salt and freshly-ground black pepper
grated zest of half a lemon
½ inch (1cm.) piece fresh ginger, finely chopped
4–5 fl. oz. (125–150ml.) Noilly Prat vermouth

This recipe is equally successful baked in a foil-covered dish, served perhaps with a light beurre blanc (see page 101) made with the cooking juices.

Trim the fish and divide into six portions. Cut the vegetables into julienne strips and blanch for one minute in boiling water, refresh and drain.

Place the fish on the buttered greaseproof paper and season lightly. Strew the vegetables, lemon zest and ginger over each one, then add a splash of Noilly Prat.

Join the paper edges and fold several times, tucking in the ends to trap the steam. Place the parcels on a baking sheet and bake at 400F/200C/Gas 6 for 5–7 minutes depending on the thickness of the fish.

Take the parcels straight from the oven to the table, setting each one on a plate and snipping open with scissors under the guests' noses for the aroma to escape as the contents of the parcel are revealed ... Ah!

Fish à la Meunière

The Fox and Goose, Fressingfield
Chef/proprietor Adrian Clarke

Serves 1

4 oz. (125g.) butter
2 tablespoons lemon juice
1 tablespoon fresh herbs
black pepper, freshly ground
a little flour, seasoned with salt and black pepper
1–1½ lbs. (450–700g.) fish
a couple of king prawns, grilled
wedges of lemon

A la Meunière quite simply means cooking in butter, fresh lemon juice and a generous pinch of fresh, finely chopped herbs: parsley, tarragon, chervil and chives.

You can cook practically any fish 'à la meunière' but always try to get a fish weighing 1–1½ lbs. (450–700g.). Leave it on the bone but skin it. Dover Sole is perhaps the best fish for this dish.

In an oval fish pan or large frying pan place the butter, lemon juice, herbs and black pepper. Heat the butter until sizzling, dip the fish in the flour on both sides, shake off the excess and add to the pan. Reduce the heat to moderate and cook for 4 minutes on one side and the same time on the other. The fish should be golden brown. Serve on a hot plate with grilled king prawns, wedges of lemon and some of the wonderful burnt butter tipped over it. Simple and delicious!

French fries, French beans and flash-fried courgettes are particularly good with this dish.

As for wine I would plump for Pouilly Fumé, Sancerre, or Muscadet as a superb accompaniment to the fish.

Escalope of Brill with Shallots and Beurre Rouge

Teignworthy Hotel, Frenchbeer
Chef David Woolfall

Serves 2

butter for greasing
salt and freshly-ground black pepper
2 escalopes of brill
about 5 fl. oz. (150ml.) fish or vegetable stock

For the beurre rouge:

2 heaped tablespoons shallots, finely chopped
4 tablespoons good red wine
2 tablespoons red wine vinegar
4 oz. (125g.) unsalted butter, diced

Grease the bottom of a deep, non-iron pan with a little butter. Season the brill and place in the pan. Add the fish stock until it just covers the brill, cover with greaseproof paper and poach in a moderate oven for about 12–15 minutes until just cooked.

Keep the fish warm and save the cooking liquor. Add the shallots, red wine and red wine vinegar to the liquor and reduce to the consistency of syrup in a saucepan. Remove from direct heat and add the butter a piece at a time, whisking constantly until all the butter is melted. Arrange the brill on a plate, spoon over the sauce and garnish.

Fillets of Brill in Champagne

Paris House, Woburn
Chef/proprietor Peter Chandler

Serves 6

8 oz. (225g.) salmon fillet or tail-end
1 egg white
1 pint (570ml.) double cream
6 fillets of brill, boned
¼ pint (150ml.) fish stock
¼ pint (150ml.) champagne
½ oz. (10g.) butter
1 teaspoon chopped chives
salt and freshly-ground black pepper

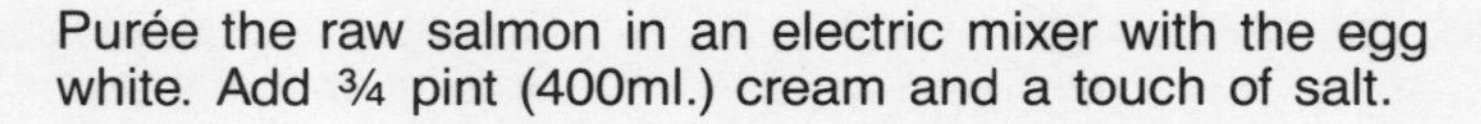
Purée the raw salmon in an electric mixer with the egg white. Add ¾ pint (400ml.) cream and a touch of salt.

Lay the brill fillets flat on a board and slice each horizontally in two, leaving a small hinge on the end. Fill the brill fillets with the puréed salmon mixture.

Fold the flap of brill back over and poach for 5 minutes in a covered pan in the fish stock and champagne with a little salt. Remove the fish from the pan and keep warm.

Reduce the liquid to a glaze and add the remaining cream. Reduce further until the sauce gives a coating consistency. Add a knob of butter to give the sauce a shine.

Add the chives at the end so that they do not discolour. Add salt and pepper. Coat the fish with the sauce and serve with a few lightly-cooked vegetables and fresh noodles.

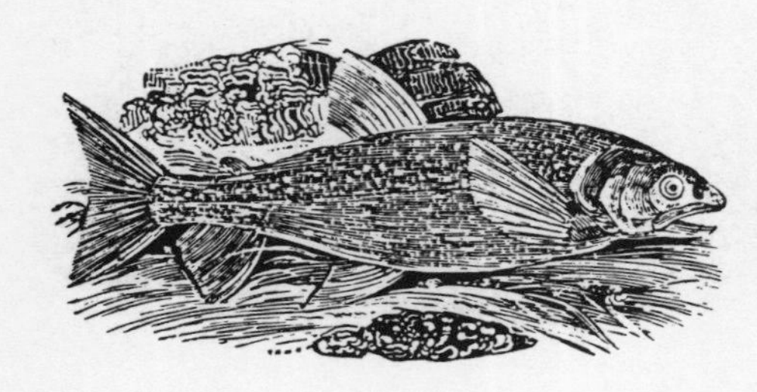

Grilled Brill with Asparagus, Sorrel and Champagne Sauce

Wolfscastle Country Hotel, Haverfordwest
Chef Michael Lewis

Serves 4

16 asparagus spears
salt
16 button onions
4 fillets of brill from a 4 lb. (1.8kg.) fish
1 oz. (25g.) melted butter, plus 3 oz. (75g.) chilled and diced butter
2 teaspoons lemon juice
freshly-ground black pepper
1 tablespoon chopped shallots
¼ bottle good dry champagne
¼ pint (150ml.) double cream
3 oz. (75g.) fresh sorrel, finely shredded
a little chopped parsley

Slice the asparagus diagonally, discarding the tough bottom ends, and boil in plenty of salted water for 4 minutes. Strain and refresh in cold water; strain again and reserve. Poach the button onions until tender, then drain them and reserve.

Brush the fillets of brill with the melted butter. Add the lemon juice and a couple of turns of the peppermill. Grill on both sides for about 4 minutes until just firm to the touch.

Keep the fillets warm and pour their juices into a saucepan. Add the shallots and champagne and reduce to about 3 tablespoons. Add the cream and reduce until smooth. Add the sorrel, simmer for 1 minute, then whisk in the diced butter a little at a time. Add the asparagus and button onions and check for seasoning.

Divide each fillet into 4 and arrange on individual plates. Pour over the sauce, arranging the vegetables attractively. Garnish with parsley.

Pavé de Cabillaud au Four, Julienne Croquante d'Artichauts à la Coriandre

Le Petit Blanc, Oxford
Chef Bruno Loubet

Serves 4

4 artichokes
1 lemon
1¼ lbs. (550g.) cod, washed, dried and cut into thick fillets
2 oz. (50g.) butter
salt and freshly-ground black pepper
curry powder
3½ oz. (100g.) carrots, peeled and cut into julienne strips
½ oz. (5g.) coriander leaves
3 small tomatoes, skinned, deseeded and diced
2 green apples
extra virgin olive oil

Cut off the artichoke stalks with a sharp knife. Remove the leaves and the hard 'choke', then cut the base into julienne strips. Add a squeeze of lemon juice.

Ten minutes before serving, pan-fry the cod, skin side first, for about 4 minutes, then place in a moderate oven until cooked.

Melt the butter in a pan on a high heat. Put in the artichokes, sprinkle with salt, pepper and a little curry powder and sauté for about 5 minutes.

Meanwhile, boil the carrots in water for 3 minutes, then add to the artichokes with the coriander leaves, tomatoes and the apples which have been cut into julienne strips.

Skin the cod and put on a hot plate. Pour over the julienne of vegetables and a spoonful of the olive oil.

Morue Fraîche à la Purée D'Ail et au Jus de Rôti

Morels, Haslemere
Chef/proprietor M. Morel

Serves 4

For the Jus de Rôti:

1 lb. (450g.) chicken bones
oil for frying
2 medium carrots, finely chopped
½ onion, finely chopped
2 cloves garlic, unpeeled
sprig of thyme
1 small bay leaf
1¾ pints (1 litre) water

2 heads garlic, peeled with the green centre removed
2 fl. oz. (50ml.) milk
3½ fl. oz. (100ml.) single cream
salt and freshly-ground black pepper
2 lbs. (900g.) fresh cod fillets

The soft garlic purée and the caramel-like juice make a wonderful contrast with the flavour and texture of the 'humble' cod. One of my favourites!

Make the jus de rôti by frying the chicken bones in a little hot oil until dark brown. Add the chopped vegetables and cook for five minutes until soft and lightly brown. Add the fresh thyme, garlic and the bay leaf and deglaze with the water. Bring to the boil, scraping the side of the pot and then simmer gently for 45 minutes. Strain and set aside. (It is always useful to keep meat bones to make a juice, which you can store in the refrigerator and use to enhance sauces as needed).

Next, make the garlic purée by putting the peeled garlic cloves in cold water to cover and bringing to the boil. Drain and refresh them and then repeat the process.

Put the garlic cloves in the milk and add the cream, salt and pepper and cook gently for 10 minutes until soft. Purée the mixture in a liquidiser or mouli.

Bake the cod fillets, add salt and pepper but not fat. When cooked, arrange on a serving plate surrounded by the garlic purée.

Boil the jus, check the seasoning and pour around the purée. Serve.

Roast Cod Steaks with Mussel and Sea-urchin Sauce

Longueville House, Mallow
Chef John Sheedy

Serves 4

4 cod steaks
2 oz. (50g.) butter
a little flour

For the sauce:

24 mussels (for preparation see page 52)
8 fl. oz. (225ml.) fish stock
4 fl. oz. (125ml.) Noilly Prat
12 sea-urchins
4 oz. (125g.) butter
cream
12 oz. (350g.) spinach

Heat the butter in a pan. Flour the cod steaks, brown them in the butter and cook in a moderate oven.

To prepare the sauce, cook the mussels in the fish stock and Noilly Prat. Remove the mussels from their shells and reserve. Remove the corals from the sea-urchins and mix with the butter. Reduce the cooking liquid and add a little cream together with the sea-urchin and butter mixture. Toss the spinach in a little melted butter.

Place the cod in the centre of a plate. Reheat the mussels in the sauce, pour the sauce around the fish and decorate with the spinach.

Fillet of Gurnard with Brioche Crumbs and Herbs and a White Wine and Red Shallot Sauce

Oakes Restaurant, Stroud
Chef/proprietor Chris Oakes

Serves 4

For the sauce:

4 medium shallots, finely chopped
red wine
Crème de Cassis
½ pint (275ml.) fish stock
3 fl. oz. (75ml.) dry white wine
½ pint (275ml.) double cream
2 oz. (50g.) unsalted butter
salt and freshly-ground white pepper

4 × 6 oz. (175g.) fillets of gurnard
salt and white pepper
¼ pint (150ml.) dry white wine
a mixture of fresh parsley, chervil, chives and tarragon, finely chopped
brioche crumbs
knob of butter

To make the sauce, place the shallots in a small saucepan and cover with a little red wine. Gently boil down the wine until there is almost no liquid remaining. Add half the amount of crème de cassis as there was red wine and gently boil down again. Reduce until hardly any of the liquid remains. Keep to one side.

Reduce the fish stock by three-quarters and add the white wine. Reduce further by half, add the cream and reduce again by half. Take off the heat and quickly whisk in the butter. Season with salt and freshly-ground white pepper and keep warm.

Place the fillets of gurnard in a thick-bottomed, shallow-sided pan and add salt and freshly-ground white pepper. Add enough white wine to cover the bottom of the pan. Cover the fish with kitchen foil and place in a pre-heated oven at 425F/220C/Gas 7 for about 8 minutes.

Take out of the oven and sprinkle with the herbs and brioche crumbs. Place a small knob of butter on the top and place under the grill until the crumbs start to turn golden brown.

Place the fish on a warmed plate with the shallots around it. Pour the sauce around the fish and serve immediately.

Hake Vercruzana

Gibson's, Cardiff
Chef/proprietor Irene Canning

Serves 6

2½ fl. oz. (60ml.) olive oil
6 cutlets of hake
2 medium onions, finely sliced
3 cloves garlic, crushed with salt
1 or 2 Jalapeno chillies, seeded and sliced. If you can not get these, use Indian chillies and half a green pepper
1½ lbs. (700g.) tomatoes, peeled, seeded and finely chopped
1 tablespoon drained capers
1 bay leaf
2 oz. (50g.) sliced stuffed olives
salt and freshly-ground black pepper
2 lemons or limes
tomato juice (optional)
fresh coriander leaves, chopped, to garnish

Heat the oil in a large frying pan and seal the fish quickly on both sides. Remove the fish, drain and arrange in a large casserole in one layer. Cook the onions in the oil in the frying pan until soft. Add the garlic and chillies, cook a moment or two longer and then add the tomatoes, capers, bay leaf and olives. Season lightly with salt and pepper. Cook for 10 minutes. Taste and adjust seasoning, adding a good squeeze of lemon or lime juice. If the tomatoes were not very juicy, you may add some tomato juice.

Pour the sauce over the fish and bake in the oven 400F/200C/Gas 6 for 15–20 minutes, depending on the thickness of the fish. Serve, garnished with chopped coriander, new potatoes cooked in their skins and a wedge of fresh lemon or lime.

Halibut with Grapes

Hope End, Ledbury
Chef/proprietor Patricia Hegarty

Serves 4–6

2 lbs. (900g.) fresh halibut, skinned and filleted
butter
freshly-ground black pepper
4 fl. oz. (125ml.) white wine
12 oz. (350g.) black grapes, peeled, deseeded and cut in half lengthwise
fresh chervil sprigs

For the Hollandaise sauce:

3 tablespoons cider vinegar
2 tablespoons water
1 bay leaf
10 black peppercorns
3 egg yolks
6 oz. (175g.) unsalted butter, melted
lemon juice
sea salt

This recipe is derived from the classic Sole Véronique. I use black grapes instead of green because, when peeled, they present an attractive rosy tinge.

Cut the fish into neat blocks about 1½ inches (3cm.) square. Line a medium-sized roasting tin with buttered foil, allowing sufficient to draw over the top and lay the pieces of fish on this, not quite touching. Brush the fish with melted butter and grind over a little black pepper. Pour the wine round the fish, fold over the foil and bake at 375F/190C/Gas 5 for 15–20 minutes.

To make the Hollandaise sauce, reduce the vinegar, water, bay leaf and peppercorns in a small pan to 1 tablespoonful. Strain and put into a processor with the egg yolks and process for 30 seconds. Slowly add the melted butter until the sauce thickens. Add a good squirt of lemon juice and salt to taste. Keep the sauce in a china pudding basin.

Just before serving, warm the sauce over some hot, but not boiling, water and gently heat the grapes in a small sauce-pan. Put a spoonful of sauce on each plate, arrange the fish and the grapes in a geometric pattern on this and decorate with chervil.

Flétan à la Fondue d'Agrumes et d'Huile d'Olive

Provence at the Gordleton Mill, Lymington
Chef/proprietor Jean-Pierre Novi

Serves 6

1 halibut, about 4 lb. (1.8kg.) skinned and filleted
3 oranges
3 lemons
salt
1 onion, chopped
bay leaves
2 teaspoons red wine vinegar
freshly-ground black pepper
4 fl. oz. (125ml.) white wine
1 small shallot, chopped
butter
Curacao
about 3 tablespoons olive oil
fresh dill, finely chopped

Cut the halibut into six portions. Peel the oranges and lemons, being careful not to take any pith, cut the peel into thin slices and blanch. Remove the pith from the oranges and lemons and divide the fruit into segments, reserving any juice as you do so.

Salt a pan of water, add the onion, bay leaves, vinegar, and one turn of the pepper mill. Bring to the boil and keep at a steady simmer.

Reduce the white wine with the shallots in a saucepan. Add the juice of the oranges and continue to reduce. Thicken the sauce by adding a little butter. Do not boil. Add the sliced orange and lemon peel and a few drops of Curacao. Sprinkle the fruit segments with the olive oil and warm under the grill for 30 seconds.

Steam the fish in a large sieve over the boiling water for a few minutes. Cover the pan but make sure that the fish is always above the water.

Arrange the fish, fruit segments and the reduced sauce on warm plates. Decorate with the dill and slices of fresh, blanched peel.

Baked Halibut in Filo Pastry

Corse Lawn House Hotel, Corse Lawn
Chef/proprietor Baba Hine

Serves 4

2 lbs. (900g.) halibut fillet
4 oz. (125g.) melted butter
salt and freshly-ground black pepper
4 fennel fronds
8 sheets of filo pastry, about 6–7 oz. (175–200g.)
Hollandaise sauce, to serve (see page 112)

Divide the halibut into four portions. Brush the portions with half the melted butter, season with salt and pepper and lay a small frond of fennel on each portion.

Brush each sheet of filo with melted butter. Using 2 sheets for each portion, wrap the fish in the filo, tucking the ends in firmly. Cook in a hot oven, 425F/220C/Gas 7 for about 8 minutes.

Serve with the Hollandaise sauce.

Grilled Herrings with Apple and Horseradish Sauce

Carved Angel, Dartmouth
Chef/proprietor Joyce Molyneux

Serves 4

4 herrings about 6–8 oz. (175–225g.) each, heads removed and gutted
seasoned flour

For the sauce:

8 oz. (225g.) cooking apples, peeled, cored and sliced
1 oz. (25g.) butter
2 teaspoons grated fresh horseradish

Roll the herrings in the seasoned flour and grill for about 5 minutes each side.

To make the sauce, cook the apples in the butter until soft and mash them to a purée. Add the horseradish and mix well.

Serve the herrings with the apple and horseradish sauce and boiled potatoes.

John Dory with Chambéry and Orange

Gibson's, Cardiff
Chef/proprietor Irene Canning

Serves 2

2½ oz. (60g.) unsalted butter, at room temperature, plus extra for greasing
1½–2 lbs. (700–900g.) John Dory, filleted, but not skinned
4 thin slices of orange
salt and freshly-ground black pepper
3 fl. oz. (75ml.) Chambéry vermouth
zest of remainder of orange, blanched 3 times to remove bitterness and cut into julienne strips

Butter an ovenproof gratin dish and put in the fillets, skin down. Top with orange slices, slightly overlapping them. Lightly season with salt and pepper and pour the vermouth around the fish. Cover with foil.

Bake in the oven 375F/190C/Gas 5 for 15–20 minutes until the fish under the orange has turned from opaque to white. Keep the fish warm and pour off the juice into a small saucepan. Boil the liquid fast to reduce to half the quantity and drop in the butter in small cubes. Whisk quickly over a low heat until the butter has melted but on no account let the sauce boil. Remove from heat, check seasoning and pour the sauce around the fish on plates. Garnish with the orange zest.

John Dory Wrapped in Cos Lettuce with a Lime and Butter Sauce

Flitwick Manor, Flitwick
Chef Geoffrey Welch

Serves 4

8 outer leaves from a Cos lettuce
4 × 6 oz. (175g.) John Dory fillets, skinned
8 tablespoons fish fumet
2 glasses dry white wine
4 shallots, finely chopped
salt and freshly-ground black pepper
knob of unsalted butter

For the sauce:

2 teaspoons finely chopped shallot
juice from 1 lime
5 tablespoons dry white wine
2 tablespoons double cream
5 oz. (150g.) chilled unsalted butter, diced
finely grated zest of 1 lime
salt and black pepper

Wash the Cos leaves in cold water, blanch and refresh. Lay the leaves out, slightly overlapping. Lay each fish fillet across two lettuce leaves and wrap up tightly. Pour the fish fumet and white wine into a gratin dish with the John Dory on top, sprinkled with the shallot. Season with salt and pepper, add a knob of butter to each portion and cover with buttered greaseproof paper. Bake in a moderate oven for 10–12 minutes and serve with the sauce.

To make the sauce, place the shallot, lime juice and white wine in a small saucepan. Boil and reduce until about 1 tablespoon of liquid remains. Add the cream and boil until the sauce begins to thicken. Reduce heat to very low and whisk in the butter a piece at a time. Add the lime zest and salt and pepper to taste.

Sautéed Monkfish Cheeks with a Red Pepper Dressing

Seafood Restaurant, Padstow
Chef/proprietor Rick Stein

Serves 4

16 monkfish cheeks or about 2 lbs. (900g.) monkfish fillet, cut into 3 inch (7.5cm.) × 1 inch (2.5cm.) pieces
2 red peppers, cut in half lengthways with seeds removed
1 fl. oz. (25ml.) olive oil, plus extra for greasing
½ pint (275ml.) fish stock
1 large pinch saffron
salt and freshly-ground black pepper
1½ teaspoons red wine vinegar

Monkfish is sold headless in England which is a pity because the cheeks are, in my opinion, the best part of the fish, being sweet in taste and firm in texture. Just occasionally, you can buy monkfish cheeks here but if you can't get them, use monkfish fillet cut into pieces.

Remove the skin and membrane from the monkfish and dry the pieces with kitchen paper. Brush a grilling tray with olive oil and flatten the peppers. Brush the skins with oil and cook them under a preheated grill until the skin is black and blistering. Remove from the grill, leave to cool then skin them. Cut the flesh into very small dice.

Put the fish stock into a small pan, add the saffron and reduce by about three-quarters. Take a thick-bottomed solid frying pan and heat until smoking hot. Brush the bottom of the pan quickly with a little olive oil and place half the monkfish in it. Season well with salt and pepper, cook on one side until golden brown then turn over with a palette knife and cook on the other side. Take out the pieces of monkfish and keep warm. Reheat the pan until smoking hot again, brush with olive oil and cook the second batch in the same way. Provided the monkfish is fresh, you should be able to cook it without sticking. Add the finely diced peppers to the reduced fish stock, bring to the boil and add the olive oil and vinegar. Season with a large pinch of salt and some pepper. Boil vigorously and whisk to emulsify the sauce. Pour the sauce on to four warmed plates and lay the monkfish on top.

Brochette de Lotte au Bacon Fumé, Sauce à l'Ail

Morels, Haslemere
Chef/proprietor J. Morel

Serves 4

2 lbs. (900g.) monkfish (tail fillet)
1 lb. (450g.) smoked streaky bacon
1 onion, peeled and cut into 4 wedges
9 oz. (250g.) butter, diced
1 clove garlic and 4 oz. (125g.) parsley chopped finely together to make a persillade
salt and freshly-ground black pepper

For the marinade:

2 tablespoons olive oil
2 tablespoons white wine
3 coriander seeds, crushed

The crisp bacon and meaty texture of the monkfish make a wonderful contrast. Try this dish on a sunny day as it makes a good barbecue dish and serve with a side salad or wild rice.

Cut up the monkfish into 1½ inch (3.5cm.) cubes and put in a bowl with the marinade. Cover the bowl and leave in the refrigerator for 2–3 hours so that the flavours mingle.

Wrap each piece of fish in a rasher of bacon. Now, alternately thread the monkfish and a curl of onion taken from the wedges on to skewers (wooden ones are best).

Make the garlic butter sauce by putting 2 tablespoons of water to warm on a low heat and then add the butter, whisking in a little piece at a time, until the mixture becomes lukewarm and creamy. Whisk constantly and never let the sauce get too hot. Remove from the heat and add the persillade. Check the seasoning.

Grill the brochettes, for a few minutes only, under a high heat. Pour the sauce over the brochettes and serve.

Monkfish Poached in Pernod with Prawns

Kirkby Fleetham Hall, Kirkby Fleetham
Chef Ray Sharp

Serves 4

1½ lbs. (700g.) monkfish tails, cut into small escalopes
½ pint (275ml.) fish stock, well seasoned
2 oz. (50g.) leeks
2 oz. (50g.) carrots
half an onion
2 oz. (50g.) bulb fennel
1 oz. (25g.) butter
½ teaspoon crushed garlic
2 oz. (50g.) tomato purée
8 large prawns
2 fl. oz. (50ml.) Pernod

Poach the monkfish in the seasoned fish stock for 5 minutes. Drain, cover and keep warm.

Cut the leeks, carrots, onion and fennel into julienne strips. Melt the butter in a saucepan and add the vegetables and garlic. Cook for two minutes without letting them colour. Add the tomato purée, prawns, Pernod and fish stock and bring all the ingredients to the boil.

Now place the monkfish in the pan and boil for a further 2 minutes.

Arrange the monkfish in a circle on a plate with the prawns in the centre. Pour the sauce over the fish and serve.

Timbales of Monkfish and Mussels with Fresh Tomato Sauce

Polmaily House Hotel, Drumnadrochit
Assistant Chef Barbara Drury

Serves 6

- 1½ lbs. (700g.) monkfish tails, trimmed and cut into strips
- 3 tablespoons olive oil
- 3 cloves garlic, peeled and thinly sliced
- 8 leaves of fresh basil, shredded
- ½ teaspoon salt
- 2 egg whites
- ½ pint (275ml.) double cream
- 3 tablespoons Noilly Prat
- 1 pint fresh mussels
- 1 lb. (450g.) fresh spinach, washed and trimmed

Marinate the monkfish overnight in the olive oil, garlic and basil. Next day remove the monkfish and reserve the marinade for the sauce. Blend the monkfish with the salt in a food processor until smooth. Add the egg whites and process for a further 2 minutes. Pass through a sieve, then add the double cream and 2 tablespoons of the Noilly Prat.

Scrub the mussels (see page 52) and cook in a heavy-based pan, tightly covered, with the poaching ingredients for about 5 minutes until opened. Remove the mussels from their shells and, when cool, add the remaining Noilly Prat to the drained mussels.

To make the sauce, sweat the shallots and carrots in the marinade liquor and olive oil for 5 minutes. Add the tomatoes, wine and seasoning. Cover and simmer gently for 30–45 minutes. Blend, then sieve.

For poaching:

¼ pint (150ml.) white wine
2 cloves garlic, unpeeled
3 sprigs of parsley

For the sauce:

2 shallots, peeled and finely chopped
1 carrot, peeled and chopped
1 tablespoon olive oil
1½ lbs. (700g.) tomatoes, quartered
¼ pint (150ml.) white wine
salt and freshly-ground black pepper

Blanch the spinach in boiling water for 1 minute. Drain and refresh. Use the leaves to line 6 individual moulds, allowing the leaves to hang over the sides. Fill the moulds two-thirds full with the monkfish mixture. Make a well in the centre and fill with mussels. Cover with more monkfish and fold the spinach leaves over the top. Cook in a bain-marie in a moderate oven for 12 minutes. Turn out on to plates and serve surrounded by the sauce.

Lotte à la Bourguignonne

Paris House, Woburn
Chef/proprietor Peter Chandler

Serves 6

1½lbs. (700g.) monkfish
6 fl. oz. (175ml.) red wine
2 shallots, chopped
butter
12 button onions
2 oz. (50g.) button mushrooms, cut into quarters
2 oz. (50g.) bacon, cut into 1 inch (2.5cm) pieces
6 fl. oz. (175ml.) fish stock
6 fl. oz. (175ml.) beef stock
6 fl. oz. (175ml.) double cream
salt and freshly-ground black pepper
12 oz. (350g.) cooked noodles

Soak the monkfish in the red wine for four hours. Cook the fish with the chopped shallots in hot butter until slightly brown. Lift out and keep warm.

In another pan, lightly brown the whole onions in some hot butter. Add the button mushrooms and bacon. Add the red wine to the juices in the pan. Add the fish stock and beef stock and reduce by half. Add the cream, bring to the boil and add salt and pepper.

Warm the fish through and lay on a bed of freshly-cooked noodles. Pour the sauce over the fish and around the vegetables.

Pollack Fillet with Orange, Lemon Grass and Ginger

Corse Lawn House Hotel, Corse Lawn
Chef/proprietor Baba Hine

Serves 4

2 lbs. (900g.) pollack fillet, cut into 4 portions (or cod if pollack is unavailable)
4 oz. (125g.) butter
peel of one orange, cut into julienne strips
2 sticks of fresh lemon grass, very finely chopped
large pinch of finely chopped root ginger
2 fl. oz. (50ml.) white wine
2 fl. oz. (50ml.) fish stock
salt and freshly-ground black pepper

Sauté the pollack for 30 seconds in 2 oz. (50g.) butter with the orange peel, lemon grass and ginger. Add the wine, stock, salt and pepper, and poach for a few minutes.

Remove the pollack when just cooked, boil the sauce for a few seconds and beat in the remaining 2 oz. (50g.) butter to thicken. Pour the sauce around the fish fillets and serve.

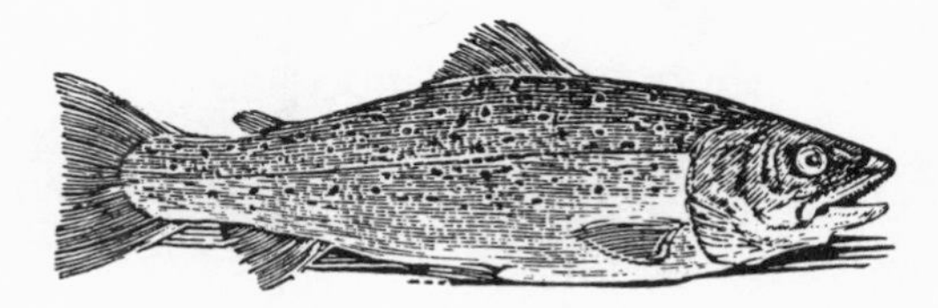

Red Mullet with Anchovy and Orange Sauce

Whites Restaurant, Cricklade
Chef/proprietor Colin White

Serves 6

6 small red mullet, scaled and cleaned

For the sauce:

8 anchovy fillets
juice of 3 oranges
8 oz. (225g.) butter, chilled and diced
grated zest of 1½ oranges
pinch of sugar

concassé of fresh ripe tomatoes, for decoration (optional)

Pound the anchovy fillets to a paste, add the orange juice and reduce by two-thirds. Whisk in the cold butter, little by little, over a very gentle heat, adding the last 1 oz. (25g.) off the heat to stop the sauce cooking. Add the orange zest and sugar to taste.

Grill or steam the fish for about 6–7 minutes each side and serve on a pool of the sauce with the tomato garnish.

As a variation you can use basil instead of the anchovies, in which case shred it and add at the last moment; a few shelled mussels also make a good garnish.

Fillet of Red Mullet with Red Wine, Chives and Green Peppercorns

Corse Lawn House Hotel, Corse Lawn
Baba Hine

Serves 4

4 red mullet, 8–10 oz. (225–275g.) each
2 oz. (50g.) butter

For the sauce:

4 fl. oz. (125ml.) red wine
4 fl. oz. (125ml.) fish stock
1 teaspoon chives, chopped
1 teaspoon soft green peppercorns
salt and freshly-ground black pepper

Fillet and bone the red mullet and make a stock with the bones. Sauté the fillets in butter for a minute or two on either side. Remove from the pan and keep warm.

Add the red wine and stock to the pan juices and reduce by half.

Add the chives and peppercorns and season to taste. Pour the sauce over the mullet fillets and serve.

Fillet of Red Mullet Baked with Braised Onion, Tomato and Thyme and Served on a Rosti Potato with a Cream Sauce

Oakes Restaurant, Stroud
Chef/proprietor Chris Oakes

Serves 4

2 lbs. (450g.) red mullet, scaled and filleted, leaving the skin on
vegetable oil, for cooking
4 large onions, peeled and finely sliced
salt and freshly-ground black pepper
1 sprig of fresh thyme
2 tomatoes, peeled, deseeded, and diced
½ pint (275ml.) fish stock
6 fl. oz. (175ml.) dry white wine
½ pint (275ml.) double cream
2 oz. (50g.) unsalted butter
freshly-ground white pepper
2 large new potatoes

Fish stock can be replaced by adding 4 fl. oz. (125ml.) of dry vermouth to the white wine when making the sauce but increase the butter by a further 2 oz. (50g.) to mellow the sauce. Ask your fishmonger to prepare the fish and to take out the small bones in the fillets.

Put a thick-bottomed pan on a high heat and add just enough vegetable oil to cover the bottom of the pan. Add the onions and stir. Reduce the heat to moderate, place a close-fitting lid on the pan and leave to stew for 5–10 minutes. Take off the lid and the onions should have started to caramelize. Add a little cold water and mix into the onions, taking up any sediment in the pan. Repeat until the onions are soft and brown and most of the liquid has evaporated. Add salt and freshly-ground pepper to taste. Remove from the heat and keep to one side.

Pick off the leaves of thyme and add to the diced tomato. Put to one side.

Boil the fish stock down gently until it has reduced by three-quarters. Add 3 fl. oz. (75ml.) of white wine and reduce further by three-quarters. Add the ½ pint (275ml.) of double cream and gently reduce again by three-quarters. Take off the heat and whisk in the butter until emulsified. Season with a little salt and ground white pepper. Keep warm.

Peel and grate the potatoes on a cheese grater and dry in a clean tea-towel. Place a small thick-bottomed frying pan over a moderate heat and add enough vegetable oil to coat the bottom of the pan. Put in a quarter of the potato and spread out so that it covers the bottom of the pan. Gently fry until golden brown on both sides. Repeat so that you have four potato 'cakes'. Keep warm.

Place the braised onion in a thick-bottomed, shallow-sided pan in four equal portions. Place the fish on top and sprinkle with the tomato and thyme mixture. Season with salt and pepper and add the remaining white wine to the pan (there should be enough liquid to cover the bottom). Cover with kitchen foil and place in a pre-heated oven at 425F/220C/Gas 7 for about 10–15 minutes. Take out when cooked and keep warm.

To serve, place each potato 'cake' on the middle of a warmed plate. Using a fish slice, scoop up the fish and onions and put on top of the potato. Pour the sauce around the fish and serve immediately.

Escalopes of Salmon with a Sorrel and Basil Sauce

Seafood Restaurant, Padstow
Chef/proprietor Richard Stein

Serves 4

1½ lbs. (700g.) salmon fillet from a good sized salmon
groundnut oil
salt
10 fl. oz. (275ml.) well-flavoured fish stock or a light chicken stock
1 tablespoon white wine vinegar
1 medium onion chopped
10 sweet basil leaves (or 20 bush basil leaves)
20 sorrel leaves
4 spinach leaves
1 teaspoon soya sauce
2 oz. (50g.) unsalted butter, diced
2 fl. oz. (50ml.) double cream
3 fl. oz. (75ml.) yoghurt

The sauce for this dish is only gently warmed through so that the fresh, herby flavours are not driven off.

Remove any bones in the fillet of salmon with a pair of tweezers or long-nosed pliers or by trapping them between your thumb and the point of a sharp knife. With a sharp filleting knife or carving knife, cut the salmon into 12 diagonal slices about ¼ inch (0.5cm.) thick, in the same way as you would cut thick slices of smoked salmon, i.e. cutting on the slant down to the skin.

Brush a grilling tray with oil and place the 12 escalopes of salmon on it. Brush them lightly with oil and season lightly with salt.

Place the stock, white wine vinegar and chopped onion in a small pan, bring to the boil and reduce the liquid by about three-quarters. Put all the other ingredients in a liquidiser and add the reduction, complete with onions. Liquidise at top speed until smooth. You don't need to sieve the sauce; a few flecks of darker green are fine. Turn out and keep cool until required.

Put the fillets under a preheated grill. You don't need to turn them; they are done when the flesh changes colour from dark pink to light pink (about 30 seconds). Reheat the sauce gently until lukewarm, then pour it over four warmed plates. Carefully lift the escalopes off the grilling tray with a palette knife and lay them on the plates, slightly overlapping.

Crown of Fresh Salmon with Lemon Sole

Fischer's, Baslow
Chef/proprietor Max Fischer

Serves 4

4 oz. (125g.) fresh salmon per person
1 medium-sized fillet of lemon sole per person

For the sauce:

3½ fl. oz. (100ml.) white wine
3½ fl. oz. (100ml.) Noilly Prat
4 shallots, finely chopped
2 oz. (50g.) unsalted butter
7 fl. oz. (200ml.) double cream
juice of 1 lemon
fresh chives

Cut each fillet of sole lengthwise and the salmon into four strips. Take one strip of sole and two of salmon and, with the salmon on either side, 'plait' the fish. As the strips are used up, work in the remaining three strips. Form the plait into a circle and set aside. Continue until you have four 'crowns'.

To make the sauce, put the white wine, Noilly Prat and shallots into a pan, simmer and reduce to about two-thirds of their original quantity.

Meanwhile, lightly steam the crowns; transfer with a spatula on to hot plates and keep warm in the oven.

Liquidise the sauce with the unsalted butter. Return to the pan, reheat and stir in the cream and lemon juice. Spoon the sauce on to each plate around the crown and sprinkle with the chives. Serve with new potatoes and a side salad.

Wild Scottish Salmon with Smoked Salmon, Leek and Crayfish Sauce

Handsels, Edinburgh
Chef Andrew Radford

Serves 10

10 × 6 oz. (175g.) wild salmon fillets
peanut oil
salt and freshly-ground black pepper
6 tablespoons lemon vinegar or white wine vinegar
12 tablespoons white wine
1 teaspoon saffron stamens or 2 packets saffron powder
½ pint (275ml.) double cream
4 crayfish tails, shelled and finely diced
4 oz. (125g.) unsalted butter, chilled and diced
10 thin slices smoked salmon
4 oz. (125g.) leek, cut into julienne strips, blanched and refreshed
parsley and chives, finely chopped

Place the salmon fillets on a tray lightly brushed with peanut oil. Brush the fish with more oil and season.

To prepare the sauce, place the vinegar, white wine and saffron in a thick-bottomed pan and reduce by half. Add the cream and diced crayfish and boil rapidly until the sauce has reduced to the consistency of custard. Remove from the heat.

Place the salmon under a hot grill for a few minutes each side until just cooked. Do not overcook. Return the sauce to the heat and, whisking continuously, add the cold diced butter. Allow the sauce to boil and then remove from the heat. If you consider the sauce to be too thick, add a little warm cream; if too thin, add a little more butter but do not reboil.

Arrange one salmon fillet in the centre of each plate. Pour a little sauce across the middle, then arrange a loose swirl of smoked salmon on top and lastly the julienne of leek. Flash under a hot grill to heat the leek. Sprinkle with finely chopped parsley and chives and serve immediately.

Butterfly of Salmon with Langoustines

Holdsworth House, Halifax
Chef Eric Claveau

Serves 4

2 oz. (50g.) butter
2 shallots, finely chopped
4 × 5 oz. (150g.) salmon steaks
3½ fl. oz. (100ml.) white wine
11 fl. oz. (300ml.) fish stock
11 fl. oz. (300ml.) single cream

For the langoustine sauce:

3 oz. (75g.) butter
4 shallots, chopped
20 langoustines, heads removed but reserved and crushed
1 tablespoon tomato purée
3½ fl. oz. (100ml.) white wine
18 fl. oz. (500ml.) fish stock
2 oz. (50g.) tomatoes, seeded and diced
1 sprig of thyme
2 sprigs of fresh tarragon
11 fl. oz. (300ml.) single cream
dash of olive oil

To make the sauce, put 1 oz. (25g.) butter in a saucepan, add the shallots and sweat. Add the crushed langoustine heads and the tomato purée and sweat again. Add the white wine, fish stock, tomato, tarragon and thyme and simmer for 30 minutes. Pass the sauce through a fine muslin, return to the pan, add the cream and reduce. Keep aside.

In the meantime, grease an oven dish with ½ oz. (10g.) butter, add the shallots and arrange the four salmon steaks on top. Season and add the white wine and fish stock; cover and poach in a moderate oven.

Peel the langoustine tails. Heat ½ oz. (10g.) butter with a little olive oil and cook the langoustine tails briefly over a brisk heat. Drain and keep hot.

When the salmon is cooked, remove from the dish and keep warm. Reduce the cooking liquor and pass through a sieve. Add the cream and reduce. Gradually whisk the remaining 1½ oz. (40g.) butter into the sauce to thicken, then keep warm while you do the same to the langoustine sauce.

To serve, cover one half of each plate with the langoustine sauce, then the other half with the second sauce. Skin and bone the salmon steaks, then quarter them. Place on the sauces to resemble butterflies and arrange the langoustine tails around them. Serve immediately.

Matelote of Fresh Salmon, Monkfish, Prawns and Mussels

Polmaily House Hotel, Drumnadrochit
Chef/proprietor Alison Parsons

Serves 4

4 pints (2.3 litres) vegetable stock, made with bulb fennel and other available fresh vegetables and herbs
½ pint (275ml.) white wine or vermouth
1 pint (570ml.) stock made with the langoustine heads
¼ pint (150ml.) liquor from the mussels
8 oz. (225g.) fresh monkfish, skinned and trimmed, cut into 8 pieces
8 oz. (225g.) fresh wild salmon, cut into 8 strips
8 large, fresh, whole langoustines, cooked and peeled
30–40 fresh mussels, already opened (see page 52)
small bunch of basil and parsley (or other fresh herbs), chopped
carrot, fennel and leek, cut into julienne strips and blanched
2 oz. (50g.) butter, chilled and diced
croûtons, to serve (optional)

Bring the combined stocks, mussel liquor and wine to the boil, turn down to barely simmering and add the monkfish. Allow to just boil, then add the salmon. Cook for about 3 minutes, then add the langoustines and mussels. Remove from direct heat. Ladle out a good 1 pint (570ml.) of the poaching liquid and boil down rapidly in another pan. Add lots of chopped parsley, half the basil strips and the julienne vegetables. Whisk in the butter to thicken slightly.

Meanwhile place 2 pieces of each fish, 2 langoustines and 6–7 mussels per person in deep bowls and when the butter has amalgamated, pour the stock over and serve immediately, topped with more basil strips and croûtons if desired.

Salmon Coulibiac

Homewood Park
Chef/proprietor Stephen Ross

Serves 8

2 lbs. (900g.) puff pastry
1 lb. (450g.) cooked rice seasoned (and flavoured with saffron in the cooking if your budget permits)
1 lb. (450g.) cooked salmon (underdone)
6 hard boiled eggs, chopped
salt and freshly-ground black pepper
handful of parsley and dill, chopped
4 oz. (125g.) butter, melted
2 egg yolks, lightly beaten, for glazing

This is a splendid looking but inexpensive salmon pie.

Roll the puff pastry into a sheet 12 × 7 inches (30.5 × 43cm.) and 1/8 inch (0.25cm.) thick. Cut off a strip 1 inch (2.5cm.) wide from the longer side and reserve for leaves or fish to decorate. On one half of the sheet make a 2 inch (5cm.) thick layer of rice followed by a layer of salmon and then the chopped egg. Top with a layer of salmon and lastly the remaining rice.

Leave a 2 inch (5cm.) border around the filling to seal the pie. Season well and strew over the herbs. Sprinkle the melted butter over the filling to moisten it.

Fold over the pastry and seal the edges with a little of the beaten eggs. Glaze the top with egg yolk and decorate with pastry fish or leaves. Glaze these too.

Bake for 20 minutes at 375F/190C/Gas 5. If the pastry is getting too coloured turn down the heat but leave it to cook a little longer.

Serve with Hollandaise sauce (see recipe page 112) or melted butter.

Salmon on a Bed of Mushrooms and Baby Onions

Longueville House, Mallow
Chef John Sheedy

Serves one

5 baby onions, peeled
butter
thyme
1 oz. (25g.) mushrooms
2 oz. (50g.) oyster mushrooms
olive oil
chives, chopped
5 oz. (150g.) escalope of wild salmon

For the sauce:

2 fl. oz. (50ml.) white wine
2 fl. oz. (50ml.) fish stock
1 fl. oz. (25ml.) cream
lemon juice
butter
chives, chopped
salt and freshly-ground black pepper

To make the sauce, reduce the white wine and add the fish stock. Reduce, add the cream and a squeeze of lemon juice and reduce again. Finish the sauce with a little butter, chives and salt and pepper. Keep warm.

Cook the baby onions in some butter with a little water and thyme. Slice all the mushrooms and toss them in some hot olive oil. Add the chives and baby onions. Lightly fry the salmon and place it on top of the vegetables in the centre of a plate. Pour the sauce around the fish.

Casserole of Wild Salmon, Monkfish and Scallops with Fresh Ginger and Basil

Woods, Bath
Chef Mary Alley

Serves 4

8 oz. (225g.) wild salmon, skinned, boned and cubed
8 oz. (225g.) monkfish, skinned, boned and cubed
12 large scallops
juice and rind of 1 lemon and 1 orange
1 small piece fresh root ginger, finely shredded
salt and freshly-ground black pepper
6 tablespoons Noilly Prat
4 shallots, finely chopped
butter
juice of 1 pink grapefruit
6 fl. oz. (175ml.) fish stock
7 fl. oz. (200ml.) double or whipping cream
1 leek, shredded and blanched
1 large carrot, cut with a cannelle knife if possible, sliced thinly and blanched
1 dessertspoon chopped fresh basil leaves

Marinate the salmon, monkfish and scallops in separate dishes, using the orange and lemon rind and juice, the ginger, salt, pepper and half the Noilly Prat.

Sweat the shallots in a little butter and add the monkfish with its marinade and the pink grapefruit juice. Cover and place in a moderately hot oven for about 5 minutes. Remove from the oven and take the monkfish out of the juice.

Add the fish stock, remaining Noilly Prat and cream to the cooking juices and bring to the boil. Reduce by a third, then add the cooked monkfish, salmon and scallops. Gently bring back to the boil and simmer for about 2 minutes. Add the leeks, carrots and basil, then taste and correct the seasoning. Serve on a bed of fresh buttered noodles.

Fillet of Sea Bass Baked in Pastry

Thornbury Castle, Thornbury
Chef Colin Hingston

Serves 6

4 oz. (125g.) salmon
1 egg white
salt and freshly-ground black pepper
4 fl. oz. (125ml.) cream
2 lbs. (900g.) puff pastry
1 sea bass about 2–2½ lb. (900g.–1kg.) skinned and filleted
ground mace
fresh herbs, chopped, or preserved ginger, chopped (optional)
2 egg yolks, beaten

Pound the salmon and egg white in a food processor until smooth. Season lightly with salt and pepper. Add the cream and mix it in. Do not over mix or the cream will turn to butter. Divide the pastry into two pieces. Further divide each piece into 9 oz. (250g.) and 7 oz. (200g.) sections. The smaller pieces are for the base and the larger for the top.

Roll out the pastry. Place one of the sea bass fillets on the pastry base and season with salt, pepper and a sprinkling of ground mace. If desired, one can sprinkle the fish with fresh herbs or preserved ginger. Cover with half the salmon mousseline. Brush the edges of the base with egg yolk. Place the larger piece of pastry on top and trim the whole parcel to resemble a fish. Keep the trimmings for 'eyes' and 'fins' to decorate. Repeat the process to assemble the second 'fish'. Paint with egg yolk and decorate. Bake in a medium oven for about 30 minutes.

Baked Sea Bass with Fennel and a Tomato and Thyme Sauce

Restaurant Nineteen, Bradford
Chef/proprietor Stephen Smith

Serves 4

butter, for cooking
4 oz. (125g.) onion, finely chopped
1 lb. (450g.) tomatoes, skinned, deseeded and roughly chopped
½ bay leaf
2 sprigs of fresh thyme
¾ teaspoon salt
freshly-ground white pepper
¼ pint (150ml.) double cream
1 large fennel bulb, cut into fairly thin slices
4 × 6 oz. (175g.) sea bass fillets or halibut steaks
4 sprigs of dill

Melt the butter in a saucepan and cook the onion until soft. Add the tomatoes, bay leaf, thyme, salt and 8 turns of the pepper mill. Cook until soft. Purée in a liquidiser or food processor, then pass through a sieve. Pour in the cream, heat gently and check the seasoning. Keep warm.

Scatter the fennel slices in an ovenproof dish large enough to take the four portions of fish. Sprinkle with salt and place the sea bass, skin side up, on top of the fennel. Brush with melted butter and cover with foil. Bake in a moderate oven for 10–15 minutes, depending on the thickness of the fish.

Pour the sauce on to the plate and place the well-drained fennel in the centre with the sea bass on top. Remove the skin if you prefer and turn the fish over. Brush with a little butter and garnish with a sprig of dill.

Medallion of Sea Bass Stuffed with a Julienne of Vegetables and Ginger, Served with a Spicy White Wine Sauce

Sharrow Bay Hotel, Ullswater
Chefs Juan Martin and Colin Akrigg and the Team of Six

Serves 6

2 lbs. (900g.) sea bass, filleted, bones and skin removed
butter
1 oz. (25g.) fresh ginger, peeled and cut into julienne strips
8 oz. (225g.) total weight of carrot, leek, celeriac and mushrooms, cut into julienne strips
a little white wine
butter
¼ pint (150ml.) crème fraîche or double cream
salt and freshly-ground black pepper

For the sauce:

4 shallots, chopped
butter
20 cardamom pods
2 star anise (optional)
1 tablespoon coriander seeds, crushed
trimmings from the ginger
black pepper
¼ pint (150ml.) white wine
½ pint (275ml.) fish stock
½ pint (275ml.) double cream
salt and black pepper
lemon juice

To prepare the stuffing, blanch the ginger in boiling water for about 5 minutes. Cook the julienne vegetables in the white wine and a little butter. When nearly cooked, add the ginger and the crème fraîche or cream. Reduce until thick and then season. Allow to cool.

Cut the sea bass into even-sized medallions. With a very sharp knife, cut a pocket in each medallion and stuff with the julienne of vegetables. Wrap each portion in foil with a flake of butter and cook in a moderate oven.

To make the sauce, sweat the shallots in a little butter. Add the spices, white wine and fish stock. Reduce by half, add the cream and reduce again to the desired consistency. Season to taste with salt, pepper and lemon juice.

Skate in Pastry with Watercress and Beurre Blanc

Carved Angel, Dartmouth
Chef/proprietor Joyce Molyneux

Serves 4

1 lb. (450g.) skate, boned
salt and freshly-ground black pepper
¼ pint (150ml.) double cream
1 bunch watercress, chopped
9 oz. (250g.) puff pastry

For the beurre blanc:

4 shallots, finely chopped
4 teaspoons butter
12 fl. oz. (350ml.) white wine
5 oz. (150g.) unsalted butter, chilled and diced
salt and freshly-ground black pepper

Dice the fish and mix with the seasoning, cream and half the watercress. Roll out the pastry about ½ inch (1cm.) thick; cut into four squares and pile some of the fish mixture on to each. Fold diagonally to make triangular parcels and bake for 18 minutes.

To make the beurre blanc, sweat the shallots in the butter. Add the wine, bring to the boil and boil rapidly until 2 tablespoons of liquid are left. Add the butter in cubes, beating well between each addition. Add the remaining watercress, very finely chopped, and season. Serve the pastries surrounded by the sauce.

Fresh Skate Layered with Spinach and Wild Mushrooms on a Cream and Chive Sauce

Calcot Manor, Tetbury
Chef Ramon Farthing

Serves 4

6 oz. (175g.) unsalted butter
salt and freshly-ground black pepper
4 medium-sized fresh skate wings
8 oz. (225g.) spinach, trimmed and washed
4 oz. (125g.) oyster mushrooms

For the sauce:

6 fl. oz. (175ml.) medium dry white wine
4 fl. oz. (125ml.) fish stock
8 fl. oz. (225ml.) chicken stock
¾ pint (400ml.) whipping cream
1 bunch fresh chives, chopped

Melt approximately 4 oz. (125g.) butter in a large frying pan until it takes on a nut-brown colour. Lightly season both sides of the wings and place in the pan. Seal both sides lightly and then place in the oven at a moderate heat to cook for about 10–15 minutes or until the flesh is tender.

To make the sauce, put the white wine, fish stock and half the chicken stock into a pan and reduce over a constant heat until it takes on the consistency of syrup. At this point, whisk in the whipping cream and bring to a very gentle simmer, whisking at intervals.

Remove the fish from the oven and allow to cool.

Melt a little butter in two pans. In one, place the remainder of the chicken stock. Put in the spinach leaves with a little seasoning and allow to braise gently until tender. In the other pan put the oyster mushrooms and cook until slightly brown.

Return to the skate and gently scrape away the outermost layer of skin on one side, then gently scrape off the flesh. Keeping the flesh in its natural segments, put into a clean saucepan and repeat the process on the other side. When all the wings have been done, pour a little of the cream sauce through a sieve on to the fish, just enough to moisten. Pass the rest of the sauce into a clean pan and leave on the edge of the stove on a gentle heat to warm through.

Put the spinach into a sieve and press hard to remove excess moisture. Place the mushrooms on kitchen paper to remove any surplus fat.

Using a 4 inch (10cm.) pastry cutter ring on a greased tray, put a layer of fish into the bottom of the cutter and press down with a spoon. Place a layer of spinach leaves on top of this, followed by a layer of mushrooms, again pressing down firmly and evenly. Finally add another layer of fish. Repeat this process with the three other portions and place in the oven to heat through. When they are hot, lift off the tray using a fish slice under the cutter and put into the centre of the serving plates. Quickly whisk a little butter into the sauce and add the chopped chives. Spoon the sauce around the fish, drizzling a little on top as well. Serve immediately.

Aile de Raie Pochée, Sauce Tartare

Le Petit Blanc, Oxford
Chef Bruno Loubet

Serves 4

2½ lbs. (1.2kg.) skate wings
6 shallots, sliced
3½ fl. oz. (100ml.) white wine
2 fl. oz. (50ml.) wine vinegar
salt and freshly-ground black pepper
3½ fl. oz. (100ml.) olive oil
2 oz. (50g.) butter, diced
juice of 1 lemon
½ oz. (10g.) parsley, finely chopped
½ oz. (10g.) chives, finely snipped
1 oz. (25g.) capers, chopped
1 oz. (25g.) gherkins, finely chopped
3 small tomatoes, skinned, deseeded and diced

Place the skate wings on top of the shallots with the white wine, vinegar, a little water and seasoning in a large, shallow, flameproof casserole. Bring to the boil, cover with a lid and cook in a moderate oven for 5–10 minutes, depending on the thickness of the fish.

Remove from the oven, drain, then place the fish on a serving dish and keep warm. Pass the cooking juices through a chinois or very fine sieve and put in a liquidiser with the olive oil, butter and lemon juice. Blend for 2 minutes.

Put the sauce back in the pan with the capers, parsley, chives, gherkins and diced tomatoes. Pour the sauce over the fish and serve.

Poached Fillets of Dover Sole on a Crayfish Butter Sauce

Crowthers Restaurant, East Sheen
Chef/proprietor Andrew Eastick

Serves 4

2 dover sole, about 1 lb. (450g.) each, cleaned, skinned and filleted
1 oz. (25g.) shallot, finely chopped
18 fl. oz. (500ml.) fish stock

For the sauce:

20 freshwater crayfish
½ oz. (10g.) shallot, finely chopped
1 clove garlic, finely chopped
2 oz. (50g.) tomatoes, chopped
few sprigs of fresh tarragon, chopped
few sprigs of fresh thyme, chopped
3½ fl. oz. (100ml.) dry white wine
18 fl. oz. (500ml.) fish stock
9 fl. oz. (250ml.) chicken stock
3½ fl. oz. (100ml.) cream
salt and black pepper
7 oz. (200g.) unsalted butter

To make the sauce, cook the crayfish in boiling water for 1 minute. Remove and cool immediately with ice and running cold water. Shell and remove the intestines that run along the length of the tail. Reserve the shells.

Melt a knob of butter in a thick-bottomed pan and sweat the shallots and garlic. Add the crayfish shells and continue to sweat, crushing the shells as they cook. Add the tomatoes and herbs and sweat for a few minutes more. Add the wine, reduce a little; add the fish and chicken stocks and simmer for 30 minutes.

Add the cream and some salt and pepper and bring the sauce to the boil. Pass the sauce through a fine chinois or muslin, return to the pan and reduce to strengthen the flavour. Whisk in the diced, softened butter little by little to thicken. Check the seasoning, adjusting if necessary.

Do not cook the sole until the sauce is almost ready to serve. Grease a shallow dish with butter and sprinkle with shallots. Lay the sole in the dish, pour on the fish stock and cover with a butter paper. Bring to simmering point over a gentle heat, then cook in a gentle oven for 3–4 minutes.

To serve, mirror 4 warm plates with the hot sauce, arrange the drained fillets of sole on top and garnish with crayfish tails. Fresh or dried, soaked morels may also be added as a garnish.

Stuffed Fillet of Dover Sole with a Lemon Sole Mousse

Lynwood House Restaurant, Barnstaple
Chef/proprietor Ruth Roberts

Serves 4

4 fillets of dover sole, skinned
a few cooked and shelled prawns for each fillet
salt and freshly-ground black pepper
a handful of coarsely chopped fresh mixed vegetables, such as carrot, onion, celery, leek

For the mousse:

1 lemon sole approximately 1–1¼ lbs. (450–550g.), skinned, filleted, then weighed
for every 8 oz. (225g.) flesh add:
2 egg whites
juice of ½ lemon
½ teaspoon salt
1 dessertspoon double cream
butter for greasing

For the sauce:

knob of butter
2 oz. (50g.) prawns
1 fl. oz. (25ml.) brandy
4 fl. oz. (125ml.) white wine
¼ pint (150ml.) whipping cream

To make the mousse, put the fish, egg whites and salt into a food processor and process until thick. Add the lemon juice and the cream and mix well. Roll the mixture in buttered tinfoil like a sausage and poach in simmering water for about five minutes. Once cooked, leave it wrapped in the foil to keep warm until needed. Now prepare the dover sole.

Wrap each fillet around a few prawns, secure with a wooden cocktail stick and poach in seasoned water into which you have thrown some coarsely chopped vegetables.

To prepare the sauce, heat the butter in a frying pan and sauté the prawns. Flambé with the brandy before adding the wine and cream. Whisk, then simmer to reduce the sauce to a pouring consistency. Place slices of mousse, and the fillets of sole covered with some prawn sauce on individual plates and glaze under the grill for a few seconds. Serve immediately.

Squid Provençale

Grafton Manor, Bromsgrove
Chef Nicola Morris

Serves 4–6

2 lbs. (900g.) squid
2 large onions, sliced
2 oz. (50g.) butter
¼ pint (150ml.) Noilly Prat
½ pint (275ml.) white wine
½ pint (275ml.) fish stock
1 × 4½ oz. (140g.) tube tomato purée
12 oz. (350g.) baby sweetcorn
1 tablespoon fresh basil, chopped, plus extra to garnish
1 tablespoon fresh lovage, chopped, plus extra to garnish
salt and freshly-ground black pepper
¼ pint (150ml.) cream

Clean the squid and remove the transparent backbone which looks like plastic. Cut off the tentacles and cut the tubes into rings. Discard the head.

Sweat the onion in butter in a large frying pan until soft and transfer to a casserole dish. Add the squid to the frying pan and cook for 5–10 minutes; the colour and texture will change to white and rubbery. Place the squid in the casserole dish.

Pour the vermouth into the frying pan and add the wine, fish stock and the whole tube of tomato purée. Stir well and pour this mixture over the squid. Add the sweetcorn and sprinkle with the herbs, salt and black pepper.

Cover with foil and cook at 400F/200C/Gas 6 for approximately 1½ hours – the squid will now be very tender. Stir in the cream to finish and adjust the seasoning. Serve immediately in a large dish, sprinkled with more fresh herbs. This dish can be stored in the refrigerator and successfully reheated the next day.

Squid and Tomato with Tagliatelle

Danescombe Valley Hotel, Danescombe Valley
Chef/proprietor Anna Smith

Serves 6 as a starter

1 lb. (450g.) squid
small knob of butter
olive oil
4–5 fresh tomatoes, peeled and finely chopped
fresh tagliatelle
salt
2 cloves garlic, crushed
2 tablespoons chopped fresh basil
freshly-ground black pepper

Cut the head off the squid, extract the transparent bone and clean the body sac thoroughly. Cut the body and tentacles up into small pieces, discarding the head. Fry gently in a little olive oil and butter in a large pan for 10 minutes. Add the tomatoes and fry for another 3–4 minutes.

Cook the fresh tagliatelle in boiling salted water until al dente (about 2–3 minutes).

Stir the garlic and 1 tablespoon of the basil into the squid mixture and season with salt and pepper.

Serve the tagliatelle with the squid and tomato sauce ladled on top and garnished with the remaining basil.

Braised Sea Trout in Red Wine with Onions

Lynwood House, Barnstaple
Chef/proprietor Ruth Roberts

Serves 2

knob of butter
2 good sized cutlets sea trout, about 7–8 oz. (200–225g.) each
1 small onion, finely sliced
4 fl. oz. (125ml.) red wine
¼ pint (150ml.) whipping cream
salt and freshly-ground black pepper
1 dessertspoon roughly chopped fresh dill

Melt the butter in a frying pan and gently cook the sea trout and onions, with the lid on, for approximately 2 minutes each side without letting the onion colour. Remove the fish from the pan, take out the bone and peel off the skin by winding around the prongs of a fork.

Add the red wine and cream, turning the heat up high, and reduce the sauce to a thick pouring consistency. Correct the seasoning and pour the sauce over the fish. Garnish with the dill and serve immediately.

Poached Cornet of Squid Filled with an Avocado Mousse and Shellfish

Bodysgallen Hall, Llandudno
Chef Martin James

Serves 4

4 small squid
1 × 1 lb. (450g.) live lobster
1 × 1½ lb. (700g.) live crab
4 live scallops
a little clarified butter
tomatoes, skinned, deseeded and finely chopped, to garnish
fresh basil sprigs, to garnish
vinaigrette, to serve

For the cooking liquor for the fish:

4 pints (2.3 litres) water
1 Spanish onion, sliced
2 bay leaves
2 fl. oz. (50ml.) white wine
1 carrot, sliced
1 bunch parsley stalks
1 oz. (25g.) juniper berries

Remove the head and innards from the body of the squid. Wash under cold water and remove the centre bone and outer transparent skin. Bring the cooking liquor to the boil. Add the squid, cook for one minute and remove. Cook the lobster for four minutes, remove and add the crab for ten minutes. The scallops should be opened from their shell, the black parts and greyish gristle cut out and discarded, then the 'cushions' cooked separately in a little hot clarified butter. Remove all the meat from the shellfish and cut up into rough dice. Also dice up the squid tentacles and mix them all together.

To make the avocado mousse, soak the gelatine in cold water. Peel the avocados and discard the stones. Blend the avocados in a food processor and add the mustard, lemon juice, salt and pepper. Remove the gelatine from its water and melt in the white wine over a gentle heat. Once melted, stir into the avocado mixture.

Combine the diced shellfish with the avocado mousse and fill each squid body with the mixture. Place in the refrigerator and allow to set.

For the avocado mousse:

5 leaves of gelatine
4 avocados
1 teaspoon Meaux mustard
juice of 1 lemon
salt and freshly-ground black pepper
2 fl. oz. (50ml.) dry white wine

Slice the squid and arrange in a half-circle cornet shape on the base of a plate. Garnish with chopped, peeled tomatoes in the centre of the plate, topped with a sprig of fresh basil. Serve with a vinaigrette sauce.

Baked Salmon Trout with a Julienne of Vegetables and Hollandaise Sauce

Pool Court, Pool in Wharfedale
Chef Melvin Jordan

Serves 4

2 sticks celery
1 small leek
2 medium carrots
3 oz. (75g.) unsalted butter
2 tablespoons chopped mixed herbs (parsley, dill, chives and chervil)
1 lemon, squeezed
4 × 6 oz. (175g.) salmon trout fillets (skinned)
salt and freshly-ground black pepper
4 tablespoons dry white wine

Wash and trim the celery and leek and peel the carrots. Cut the vegetables into very thin strips, approximately the size of matchsticks. Blend 2 oz. (50g.) of the butter with the herbs and lemon juice.

Cut four large oblongs of aluminium foil and lightly grease them with the remaining butter. Divide the vegetables into four and place in the middle of each piece of foil and then top each mound with a trout fillet. Finally add a knob of the herb butter.

Bring up the sides of the foil, lightly season the fish and add a tablespoon of wine to each parcel. Close up the foil and bake on a tray in a pre-heated oven 400–425F/200–220C/ Gas 6–7 for approximately 15–20 minutes. Open carefully and serve with a Hollandaise sauce.

Hollandaise sauce:

1 teaspoon white peppercorns, crushed
1 tablespoon white wine vinegar
3 tablespoons cold water
3 egg yolks
9 oz. (250g.) unsalted butter, melted
juice of half a lemon

If you don't want to make the sauce at the last minute you can add a tablespoon of bechamel (white sauce) to the Hollandaise which will prevent it cracking while being kept warm. If, in the making, the sauce starts to split, i.e. turn to scrambled egg, stop whisking immediately and lift off the heat. Pour one tablespoon of cold water to one side of the bowl and using very gentle whisking movements mix the egg mixture into the cold water. When it goes smooth again continue to add the melted butter, but remember not to overheat.

Mix together in a pan the peppercorns, vinegar and 2 tablespoons of the cold water. Reduce by half over a moderate heat. Remove from the heat.

Place the egg yolks and remaining water into a glass or stainless steel bowl and whisk lightly while adding the strained vinegar mixture, a little at a time, stirring well.

Place the bowl over a pan of gently simmering water and whisk continuously until the mixture is thick and creamy, (do not allow it to become too hot as it may scramble). Whisk in the butter a little at a time. If the sauce becomes too thick add a few tablespoons of lukewarm water. Season to taste and add a few drops of lemon juice. Serve as soon as possible.

Fillets of Trout en Papillote with Lemon and Ginger

Michael's, Bristol
Chef/proprietor Michael McGowan

Serves 4

3½ oz. (100g.) carrots
3½ oz. (100g.) mushrooms
3½ oz. (100g.) onion
3½ oz. (100g.) leeks
5 oz. (150g.) butter
salt and freshly-ground black pepper
1 lemon
4 tablespoons oil
1¼ lbs. (550g.) trout fillets, boned
1 teaspoon chopped shallot
fresh root ginger, peeled and cut into very fine julienne strips
8 tablespoons white wine
5 tablespoons chicken stock
fresh coriander leaves

Cut the vegetables into julienne strips, soften in 2 oz. (50g.) of the butter and season. Take the rind off the lemon and cut out the segments, reserving any juice as you do so.

To make the papillotes, brush 4 greaseproof paper rounds with oil. Place some of the vegetables on one half of each round with the trout fillets on top. Season with salt and pepper. Sprinkle with the shallot and ginger and place a couple of lemon slices on top. Dot with the remaining butter and pour over the wine, stock and lemon juice. Scatter a few coriander leaves over the top. Seal by making small, overlapping folds in the paper; give an extra last fold and secure with a paper-clip. Alternatively you may use foil for the parcels. Bake at 350F/180C/Gas 4 for 15–20 minutes. Serve immediately on a hot plate with boiled new potatoes or rice. Let your guests open their own parcels.

Stuffed Trout Fillets with a Shrimp Sauce

Holdsworth House, Halifax
Chef Eric Claveau

Serves 4

8 small trout fillets, skinned
¼ pint (150ml.) dry white wine
salt

For the mushroom duxelle:

2 shallots, finely chopped
2 oz. (50g.) butter
12 oz. (350g.) mushrooms, very finely chopped
1 tablespoon lemon juice
¼ pint (150ml.) dry white wine
salt and black pepper
1 tablespoon chopped parsley

For the sauce:

2 oz. (50g.) butter
1 tablespoon olive oil
4 shallots, chopped
7 oz. (200g.) shrimps (shell on) crushed
3½ fl. oz. (100ml.) white wine
1 small tomato, seeded and diced
few sprigs of basil
18 fl. oz. (500ml.) fish stock
11 fl. oz. (300ml.) single cream

To make the mushroom duxelle, sweat the shallots in the butter until softened. Add the mushrooms and lemon juice and heat until the moisture has evaporated. Pour in the white wine, add salt and pepper and cook again until all the liquid has completely evaporated. Mix in the parsley.

Divide the duxelle into four portions. Place each portion on top of four trout fillets and cover the duxelle with the remaining fillets, flesh side up (i.e. not the skinned side). Place in an oven dish and pour in the white wine. Salt lightly, cover the dish and poach in a moderate oven.

To make the sauce, put ½ oz. (10g.) butter with the olive oil in a saucepan, add the shallots and sweat. Add the crushed shrimps and sweat again. Add the white wine, tomatoes, basil and fish stock and simmer for 30 minutes. Pass the sauce through a muslin, add the cream and reduce to a thick pouring consistency. Gradually work in the remaining butter to thicken the sauce.

Pour the hot sauce on to each plate and place the trout fillets on top. Serve immediately.

Tuna with Cockles and Garlic Butter

Hintlesham Hall, Hintlesham
Chef Robert Mabey

Serves 4

11 oz. (300g.) soft butter
3 oz. (75g.) parsley, washed and chopped
4 cloves garlic, crushed and finely chopped
1 pint (570ml.) fresh cockles or 8 oz. (225g.) frozen
4 fl. oz. (125ml.) dry white wine
salt and freshly-ground black pepper
4 large slices fresh tuna
olive oil
12 oz. (350g.) baby spinach, well washed and trimmed

Whisk the butter, garlic and parsley together in a food processor until a light greeny-white colour and three times its volume.

Wash the cockles, then cook them in a tall pan with the white wine, covering with a lid and steaming them until all open. Shell the cockles and keep warm. Strain off any sediment through a fine muslin, then boil the juices until you have two tablespoons left. Whisk in the garlic butter a little at a time, but do not boil. Return the cockles to the pan and season.

Season the tuna and brush with oil. On a skillet, grill, stove top or dry hot pan, quickly blacken the outside, leaving the middle a little pink. Dry the spinach, then sauté in a little oil and season. Arrange on four plates with the tuna on top, then pour on the cockle and butter sauce.

Poached Fillet of Turbot with a Fresh Herb Mousseline and Whole Grain Mustard Sauce

Priory Hotel, Bath
Chef Michael Collom

Serves 6

For the mousse:

4 oz. (125g.) scallops
4 oz. (125g.) monkfish
1 egg white
salt
½ pint (275ml.) double cream
1 tablespoon basil, chopped
1 tablespoon dill, chopped
1 tablespoon tarragon, chopped
1 pint (570ml.) fish stock
½ pint (275ml.) white wine
6 fillets of turbot
salt and black pepper
¼ pint (150ml.) double cream
1 tablespoon whole grain mustard
1 large tomato (optional)
sprigs of basil, dill and tarragon, to garnish

To prepare the fish mousse, blend the scallops and monkfish with the egg white to a smooth purée and push through a sieve. Add a good pinch of salt and beat with a wooden spoon until firm and slightly rubbery. Add the double cream slowly, beating all the time. Incorporate the chopped herbs and check the seasoning. Place in the refrigerator until required.

Take a large, deep frying pan or roasting tin and pour in the fish stock and white wine. Place the turbot fillets on a board and season with salt and pepper. Using a palette knife, spread the chilled mousse evenly over the fish. It should be roughly ¼ inch (0.5cm.) deep. Carefully put the fillets into the frying pan with the mousse just above the poaching liquor. Cover with a lid or tin foil and bake gently in the oven for 10–15 minutes or until the mousseline topping is just cooked.

Remove from the pan, cover and keep warm. Reduce the cooking liquor by two-thirds and add the double cream and mustard. For extra colour you may add thin slivers of skinned and seeded tomato. Place the turbot on individual dishes and pour the sauce around (not over) the fish. Decorate with sprigs of basil, dill and tarragon.

Turbot Van Melzen

The Fox and Goose, Fressingfield
Chef/proprietor Adrian Clarke

Serves 4

4 × 6 oz. (175g.) fillets of turbot, skinned
8 oz. (225g.) peeled langoustine tails
2 oz. (50g.) butter
2 oz. (50g.) finely chopped onion
8 oz. (225g.) button mushrooms, finely sliced
½ pint (275ml.) dry white wine
½ pint (275ml.) rich fish stock
1 tablespoon port
salt and freshly-ground black pepper
16 fl. oz. (450ml.) double cream

This recipe is named after a couple of dear friends who eat nothing but fish!

The idea of all cookery must be to allow the natural flavours of the main ingredient to dominate the whole dish. This is most important in the cooking of fish. The backbone, (if you excuse the pun), of this dish is the fish stock made from the bones that are left after filleting the turbot.

Place all the stock ingredients in a very large pan with about 8 pints (4.5 litres) of water and bring to the boil; cover and simmer for three hours. You should end up with about 5 pints (2.8 litres) stock. This stock freezes extremely well.

In a large deep, frying pan rapidly bring some water to the boil. Drop the turbot and langoustines in for about 90 seconds and remove on to a plate. This drains any excess liquid from the fish so your sauce will not cloud in the final stages.

Tip the water away and in the same pan melt the butter; allow to sizzle, then add the onions, cooking them for about 1 minute without colouring. Then add the mushrooms, cooking for a further minute before adding the wine, stock, port, salt and pepper. Reduce this to about ¼ pint (150ml.) of liquid in total. Add the cream. Care is now needed!

For the stock:

bones, head and skin of turbot
1 onion, stuck with a few cloves
half head garlic, unpeeled
1 stick celery
1 head of bulb fennel
6 medium-sized carrots
½ pint (275 ml.) white wine

Bring the cream to a rapid boil. Add the turbot and langoustines back to the sauce and continue to cook until the sauce begins to coat the turbot; keep turning the turbot during this time. After adding the fish you should only cook it for a maximum of five minutes. Place the turbot on a warm plate, spoon over the sauce and decorate each plate with the langoustines.

Mange tout, french beans, runner beans, new boiled potatoes or pommes Anna accompany this dish very well.

Any Chardonnay based wine is excellent with this dish. A good Mâcon, Californian, or if it's a special occasion, (as it must be if you're eating turbot), a Puligny Montrachet.

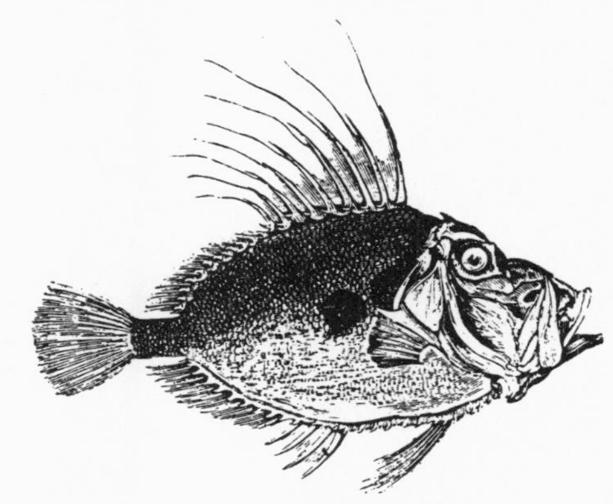

Escalope de Turbot Grillé et Jus de Veau au Romarin

L'Ortolan, Shinfield
Chef/proprietor John Burton-Race

Serves 4

4 pieces of turbot about 4 inches (10cm.) in diameter
2 medium potatoes
a little clarified butter
dill sprigs, to garnish

For the marinade:

6 fl. oz. (175ml.) hazelnut oil
zest of 1 lemon and 1 lime cut into julienne strips and blanched until tender
1 small sprig of rosemary
2 cloves garlic, sliced

For the sauce:

1 lb. (450g.) veal bones cut into small pieces, blanched and refreshed
2 large onions
1 medium carrot
¼ stick celery
1 medium leek
12 peppercorns, crushed

Place the turbot in the marinade and leave for 12 hours.

Put all the sauce ingredients except the mushrooms and rosemary in a pan and cover with water. Bring to the boil, skim and simmer gently for 8 hours. Strain, add the mushrooms and rosemary and reduce the stock until amber in colour and not too syrupy. Keep to one side until ready to use.

Slice the potatoes thinly, using a mandoline, and place a quarter of them in a small frying pan which has been brushed with clarified butter. Cook the circle of sliced potatoes until golden brown. Turn them over carefully and cook the other side, adding a few drops of clarified butter. Repeat until you have 4 galettes; place on a tray and keep warm.

Heat the reduced veal jus. Add the shallots, chives, tarragon, zests, rosemary and tomato, then whisk in the hazelnut oil. Season the jus and sharpen with a few drops of lemon juice. At the last minute, add the truffle.

Remove the turbot from the marinade and grill for about 4 minutes or until just cooked. Put to one side and keep warm.

½ clove garlic
1 sprig of thyme
½ bayleaf
1 lb. (450g.) button mushrooms, sliced
1 sprig of rosemary

To finish the sauce:

3 shallots, finely chopped
a little zest from the marinade
½ teaspoon tarragon, chopped and blanched
1 teaspoon chives, chopped
1 small sprig of rosemary
2 tomatoes, skinned, deseeded and diced into concassé
2 tablespoons of hazelnut oil from the marinade
lemon juice
1 teaspoon fine brunoise of truffle
4 oz. (125g.) foie gras, cut in ½ inch (1cm.) dice, rubbed in seasoned flour

Place the galette of potatoes in the centre of the plate, top it with the turbot and spoon the sauce with the garnish around the edge. A few lightly-cooked baby spinach leaves may be placed around the fish. Decorate with a piece of dill and finish by arranging the diced foie gras, which has been cooked in a very hot pan, around the outer edges of the plates.

Fillet of Turbot with a Pike Mousseline and White Wine Sauce

Hunstrete House, Chelwood
Chef Robert Elsmore

Serves 4

4 × 4 oz. (125g.) fillets of turbot
salt and black pepper
4 large spinach leaves, trimmed and blanched
melted butter

For the pike mousseline:

4 oz. (125g.) pike, filleted, skinned and boned
½ egg white
8 fl. oz. (225ml.) cream
salt and freshly-ground black pepper

For the white wine sauce:

½ oz. (10g.) shallot, finely chopped
1¾ oz. (45g.) butter
7 fl. oz. (200ml.) fish stock
4 fl. oz. (125ml.) Chablis
1 tablespoon Noilly Prat
4 fl. oz. (125ml.) double cream
salt and black pepper

To make the mousseline, chill the pike, then place in the food processor for 1½–2 minutes until the flesh is well pounded. Add the egg white and blend for 10 seconds. Add the cream slowly with the machine still on and blend for about 1 minute. Ensure the ingredients are evenly mixed and chill. Pass through a fine sieve, correct seasoning and place in the refrigerator until required.

To make the sauce, sweat the shallot in ½ tablespoon butter. Add the wine, fish stock and Noilly Prat and reduce almost completely. Strain through a fine sieve. Add the cream and liquidise. Cut the remaining butter into cubes, add to the sauce and liquidise. Season with salt and pepper.

Spread the mousse of pike all over one side of the turbot. Lay the fish on a steamer and cook. When the fish is just cooked, lay the blanched spinach over the top of the mousse, covering completely, and tuck the loose ends underneath the turbot. Warm the spinach through in the steamer and brush with butter so that the leaves shine nicely. Lay on a serving plate with the sauce around the fish.

Notes

Drumnadrochit
Edinburgh
Penrith
Kirkby Fleetham
Grasmere
Spark Bridge
Bradford
Pool in Wharfedale
Halifax
Baslow
Llandudno
Bromsgrove
Mallow
Diss
Corse Lawn
Ledbury
Bishop's Cleeve
Hintlesham
Haverfordwest
Thornbury
Wye
Stroud
Oxford
Woburn
Flitwick
Cardiff
Tetbury
Aston Clinton
Bristol
Bath
East Sheen
London
Cricklade
Chelwood
Sutton
Hinton Charterhouse
Shinfield
Haslemere
Barnstaple
Tunbridge Wells
Lymington
Chagford
Padstow
Calstock
Dartmouth

Restaurant Addresses

Bell Inn	– Aston Clinton, Buckinghamshire.	0296 630252
Bodysgallen Hall	– Llandudno, Gwynedd, North Wales.	0492 84466
Bridgefield House	– Spark Bridge, Nr. Ulverston, Cumbria.	0229 85239
Calcot Manor	– Nr. Tetbury, Gloucestershire.	066 689 355/227
Carved Angel	– 2 South Embankment, Dartmouth, South Devon.	08043 2465
Cleeveway House	– Bishop's Cleeve, Gloucestershire.	024 267 2585
Corse Lawn House	– Corse Lawn, Gloucestershire.	045 278 479
Crowthers	– 481 Upper Richmond Road West, East Sheen.	01 876 6372
Fischer's	– Baslow Hall, Calver Road, Baslow, Derbyshire.	024 688 3259
Flitwick Manor	– Church Road, Flitwick, Bedfordshire.	0525 712242
Fox and Goose	– Fressingfield, Diss, Norfolk.	037 986 247
Danescombe Valley	– Calstock, Cornwall.	0822 832 414
Gibson's	– 8 Romilly Crescent, Canton, Cardiff.	0222 341264
Grafton Manor	– Bromsgrove, Worcestershire.	0527 31525/37247
Handsels	– 22 Stafford Street, Edinburgh.	031 225 5521
Hintlesham Hall	– Hintlesham, Suffolk.	047 387 268
Holdsworth House	– Halifax, Yorkshire.	0422 240024
Homewood Park	– Hinton Charterhouse, Bath.	022 122 3731
Hope End	– Ledbury, Herefordshire.	0531 3613
Hunstrete House	– Chelwood, Nr. Bristol.	07618 578/579
Kirkby Fleetham Hall	– Kirkby Fleetham, North Yorkshire.	0609 748226
Longueville House	– Mallow, County Cork.	010 35322 47156
L'Ortolan	– Church Lane, Shinfield, Berkshire.	0734 883783
Lynwood House	– Bishops Tawton Road, Barnstaple, Devon.	0271 43695
Mansion House	– Mansion House Street, Dartmouth, Devon.	08043 5474
Michael's	– 129 Hotwell Road, Bristol.	0272 276190
Morels	– 23–27 Lower Street, Haslemere, Surrey.	0428 51462
Oakes	– 169, Slad Road, Stroud, Gloucestershire.	04536 79950
Paris House	– Woburn, Bedfordshire.	0525 290 692
Partners 23	– Stonecot Hill, Sutton, Surrey.	01 644 7743
Petit Blanc	– 61a, Banbury Road, Oxford.	0865 53540
Polmaily House	– Drumnadrochit, Highland.	04562 343
Pomegranates	– 94 Grosvenor Road, London.	01 828 6560

Pool Court	– Pool in Wharfedale, West Yorkshire.	0532 842288/9
Priory Hotel	– Weston Road, Bath.	0225 331922
Provence at the Gordleton Mill	– Lymington, Hants.	0590 682219
Restaurant 19	– North Park Road, Heaton, Bradford.	0274 492559
Seafood Restaurant	– Riverside, Padstow, Cornwall.	0841 532485
Sharrow Bay	– Lake Ullswater, Penrith, Cumbria.	08536 301/483
Teignworthy Hotel	– Frenchbeer, Chagford, Devon.	06473 3355
Thackeray's House	– 85 London Road, Tunbridge Wells, Kent.	0892 37558
Thornbury Castle	– Thornbury, Bristol.	0454 412647
White Moss House	– Rydal Water, Grasmere.	09665 295
Whites	– 93 High Street, Cricklade, Wiltshire.	0793 751110
Wife of Bath	– 4 Upper Bridge Street, Wye.	0233 812540
Wolfscastle Country Hotel	– Nr. Haverfordwest, Pembrokeshire.	043 787 225
Woods	– 9–13 Alfred Street, Bath.	0225 314812

Index